IPS

Decoding Corporate Camouflage

U.S. Business Support for Apartheid

Elizabeth Schmidt

Foreword by Congressman Ron Dellums

The Institute for Policy Studies is a non-partisan research institute. The views expressed in this study are solely those of the author.

Published by the Institute for Policy Studies.

Copies of this book are available from the Institute for Policy Studies, 1901 Q Street, N.W., Washington, D.C. 20009 or Paulus Potterstraat 20, 1071 DA, Amsterdam, Holland.

ISBN: 0-89758-022-2

*For the people of South Africa
in their struggle for liberation.*

ACKNOWLEDGEMENTS

Without the help and support of many friends and co-workers, this book could not have been written. I owe special thanks to Prexy Nesbitt, Robert Lawrence, Kevin Danaher, and Helen Hopps—members of the Africa Project at the Institute for Policy Studies—who provided me with invaluable insight, helpful criticism, and moral support throughout the many months of researching, writing, and rewriting the manuscript.

I sincerely thank Christine Root, of the Washington Office on Africa, and Robert Borosage, Director of the Institute for Policy Studies, for their careful reading and critiques, which contributed to the final shaping of the book.

I am indebted to the United Nations Centre Against Apartheid, which published an earlier version of the manuscript ("The Sullivan Principles: Decoding Corporate Camouflage," *Notes and Documents,* no. 4/80, March 1980), and to Beate Klein, who brought the manuscript to the Centre's attention.

The members of the Publications Program at the Institute, and Teri and Kurt Grimwood and Kathy Jungjohann, who contributed their typesetting and design skills, also deserve my special thanks.

Without the financial support of the Programme to Combat Racism of the World Council of Churches, this book could not have been published. To the Programme To Combat Racism, I am eternally grateful.

Finally, I would like to express my deepest appreciation to the nameless friends who provided me with information, materials, and patience throughout my many months of work. It is for their struggle that this book has been written.

Any weaknesses or errors in argument or presentation are my responsibility alone.

TABLE OF CONTENTS

FOREWORD

Freedom is on the march in southern Africa. It is "marching to Pretoria"—and all the other racist bastions of South Africa as well. The struggle for true freedom there—one which will liberate the oppressor as well as the oppressed—continues. It continues—and grows—despite the brutal massacres at Sharpeville and Soweto, despite the incarceration of true leaders such as Nelson Mandela, and despite the vicious murder of visionary prophets such as Steve Biko.

The Blacks in South Africa are literally a people without a country. In the land of their birth they are denied the fundamental human birthright of simple human dignity and equal justice for all, regardless of race, sex, age, or class. In the land of their birth they are classified as "migratory citizens" in almost 90 percent of their own territory, even though they comprise more than 70 percent of the nation's population.

Theirs is a world in which equal justice and fundamental human rights are held hostage to, and made victims of, the institutional madness of racism that masquerades as legality under the rubric of apartheid. What the white minority could not perpetuate through the fraudulent intellectualism of racial superiority, nor through the cultural mythology of the 'noble' "white man's burden," they now seek to sustain through systematic recourse to terror and violence, initiated and sanctioned at the highest levels of government.

The despicable acts of this apartheid government have generated increasing condemnation by the global community of conscience. This, in turn, has awakened the collective conscience of the United Nations, which has begun to speak out in the form of increased sanctions against the infamy of apartheid and its government supporters.

However, this manifestation of international concern and conscience has not deterred South Africa from continuing and even increasing its wicked ways of oppression. Sad to say, it has actually been reinforced in its determination to pursue this destructive policy in recent years because it has enlisted a new ally—the American corporate capitalist community and its gargantuan offspring, the multinational corporation. They claim to be a "progressive force" for change, in alleviating the economic misery of the Black African. The grim reality is that this has been little more than a rhetorical ruse for maximizing corporate profit margins at the expense of economic and social justice for Blacks in South Africa.

The case against corporate collaboration with institutional racism and government-sponsored violence is presented with damning documentation in this study by Elizabeth Schmidt. The author, a young scholar/journalist out of Oberlin College, who formerly worked for the Africa Project of the Institute for Policy Studies, has laid bare the hypocrisy of corporate America in paying little more than lip service to the cause of equality and justice in the South African workplace. She carefully analyzes and dissects the six "principles" in the Code for Corporate Reform there—and the results of her analysis are devastating. There is no need to hyperbolize on her part—the evidence itself is more than damning to the corporate role as well as its self-image. The actions—and deliberate inaction in some instances—of the Ford Motor Company and Citicorp (and its banking affiliate, Citibank, N.A.), to mention only two of the major transgressors, say volumes about the collective corporate immorality of American business conduct in South Africa.

Ms. Schmidt condemns with equal vigor—and rigor—the corporate attempt to rationalize away their iniquity by making positive analogies between the racial situation in the United States and that evolving in South Africa. At one point she writes:

If the civil rights problem was licked in America, they say, the same techniques should be applied in South Africa. Take down the "Jim Crow" signs. Integrate the cafeterias and toilets. Train a few more blacks for skilled positions, and condemn the practice of racial discrimination. Once again, the corporate argument falls short. In the United States, the problem of discrimination focuses on a minority of the population; in South Africa, three-quarters of the population is denied equality of opportunity—solely on the basis of race. Yet, the solutions of the 1960's have not even worked in America. The inequities of American life— poverty, hunger, unemployment, and illiteracy—are still distributed largely according to race, even though the principles of equal employment opportunity are written into U.S. law.

This study ought to be required reading for every citizen of conscience in this country, as well as for those Members of Congress who vote appropriations for the maintenance of that racist regime in the name of defending the "Free World" against the menace of Communism and "outside agitators." It should also be required reading for our Secretary of State and all those in the Executive bureaucracy charged with making the Declaration of Independence a living reality in our conduct of foreign relations, especially with those people in the Third World striving to be free.

Ronald V. Dellums
Member of Congress
8th Congressional District, California

Peter Magubane

x

INTRODUCTION

The Economic Roots of Apartheid

The parliamentary elections of 1948 were a turning point in the history of South Africa. The Nationalist Party came to power, shifting control of the white minority government from the English-speaking to the Afrikaans-speaking population. True to their campaign promises, the Nationalists began to systematize and strengthen the pattern of racial discrimination already outlined in South African law. They embarked upon a plan for the total segregation of races, instituting for each race a special program for its "separate development." They called their new policy "apartheid," which in Afrikaans means "apartness."

Under the apartheid system, the various races in South Africa are not permitted to live in the same areas. The Asian and colored (mixed race) populations are confined to ghettoes in the "white" urban and rural areas. The native black population is denied legal residency in all urban centers and all "white" rural areas. Blacks are permitted to live only in designated African homelands, which have been whittled down to 13 percent of the land. Although they constitute nearly three-quarters of the South African population, blacks are considered to be "migratory citizens" in 87 percent of the country and are denied the political and social rights automatically conferred upon the white citizenry.

While apartheid law clearly separates the black and white populations, the total segregation of the races has not been achieved. Even the master-minds of apartheid knew that, if carried to its logical conclusion, the policy of separate development would devastate the white economy. Historically, the black population has served white farmers, mining magnates, and industrialists as a plentiful supply of cheap labor. As South Africa rushed to compete for its share in the post-World War II economic boom, the necessity for black labor became even more critical. Consequently, the concept of complete apartness

1

was altered to accommodate the economic dependency of white South Africa on cheap non-white labor. Blacks were allowed into white areas, but only to work, and only on a temporary basis.*

In order to take advantage of black labor while keeping the native population under control, the Nationalist government strengthened and expanded South Africa's "influx control" laws. According to these regulations, blacks are allowed into the white areas only if they are already employed. If a black worker loses his job, he is forced to return to his homeland to await a new contract. Consisting of scattered parcels of over-populated land, devoid of mineral wealth and industrial development, the homelands cannot begin to support three-quarters of the South African population. Consequently, they serve as vast reservoirs of cheap labor for the white economy. On contract from the homelands, black workers are channeled into the areas where their labor is needed, paid what the employer is willing to pay, and sent home when the job is done. They live apart from their families eleven months out of twelve.

The monitoring and enforcement of the influx control laws required the development of an elaborate "pass" system to keep tabs on the black population. The current pass laws require that every black South African over 16 years of age carry a permit confirming his or her right to work, travel, or reside in a given area. Failure to produce a valid pass on demand is a criminal offense resulting in imprisonment and heavy fines. Since the pass laws were instituted, hundreds of thousands of blacks have been imprisoned solely for the "crime" of carrying an invalid

---

*In 1922 the Stallard Commission recommended that the black man "... should only be allowed to enter the urban areas, which are essentially the white man's creation, when he is willing to enter and to minister to the needs of the white man, and should depart therefrom when he ceases so to minister."

In 1968, Prime Minister Vorster elaborated: "It is true that there are blacks working for us. They will continue to work for us for generations, in spite of the ideal we have to separate them completely ... The fact of the matter is this: we need them, because they work for us ... but the fact that they work for us can never entitle them to claim political rights. Not now, nor in the future."[1]

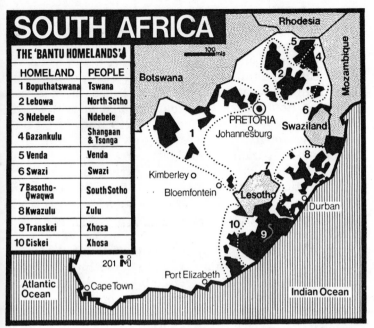

Source: International Defence and Aid Fund

pass. In 1978 alone, nearly 300,000 blacks were arrested for pass law violations.[2]

The oppressive pass system, forced migratory labor, and the strictly controlled passage of black workers into and out of the white economy are not incidental features of apartheid. Together with the laws that partitioned the country according to race, these structures constitute the fundamental building blocks of the apartheid system—a system that deprives the majority of the population of the right to own land and conduct business throughout most of South Africa. They ensure that the country's wealth, power, and privilege are concentrated in the hands of the white minority. Abhorrent racial policies dress the face of apartheid, but dispossession lies at its core.

American Business in South Africa: Agent or Obstacle to Change?

In the decades that followed the Second World War, South Africa's cheap labor economy and mineral wealth

3

attracted billions of dollars in foreign investments. Although the "good investment climate" was due, in large part, to the racist structure of the economy, the United States government adopted a "neutral" policy vis a vis American investments in South Africa.* Consequently, American corporations rapidly expanded their investments in South Africa without remonstrance from the American government. Between 1943 and 1978, U.S. direct investment in South Africa grew from $50 million to $2 billion—an increase of 4,000 percent.[4] However, as American involvement in South Africa increased, the voices criticizing corporate collaboration with apartheid grew stronger. In the United States, student groups, trade unions, religious organizations, and support groups in the black and white communities launched a nationwide campaign to sever all economic ties to South Africa. A number of international organizations, including the United Nations General Assembly, the International Labor Organization, the Organization of African Unity, and the World Council of Churches, condemned apartheid and called upon all nations to withdraw their investments from South Africa.[5]

The growing criticism from their shareholders and the mounting protests from the general public induced American businesses to prepare an argument in their defense. Although they were originally attracted to South Africa by its record of high business profits, American companies now claim that, once entrenched in the system, they serve as a "progressive force" for change. As foreign

---

*The Carter Administration reaffirmed its support of a neutral investment policy in a statement released in July 1977:

"The fundamental policy of the U.S. Government toward international investment is to neither promote nor discourage inward or outward investment flows or activities"; and, "The Government should therefore normally avoid measures which would give special incentives or disincentives to investment flows or activities, and should not normally intervene in the activities of individual companies regarding international investment."

Testifying before the Africa and International Economic Policy and Trade Subcommittees of the House of Representatives, Assistant Secretary of the Treasury, C. Fred Bergsten stressed that investments in South Africa are not exempt from the government's policy.[3]

U.S. INVESTMENTS IN SOUTH AFRICA
1943-1978

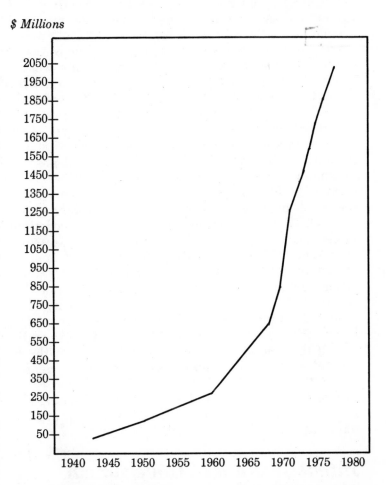

$ Millions

investments increase, they argue, so does the strength of the national economy. The benefits "trickle down" to the general population. More jobs are created. Wages inevitably rise, and on the heels of economic growth will come political and social transformation. Moreover, the corporations insist, apartheid is becoming obsolete. The expanding South African economy needs skilled labor. Blacks cannot be consigned to menial tasks forever. American businesses should remain in South Africa to provide jobs for these blacks when the economy finally needs them. Better for them to be hired by an American company with experience in equal hiring practices, than a South African firm that has always functioned inside the apartheid system.

History has exposed the weakness of the corporate argument. The "trickle down" theory has not worked. While the South African gross domestic product has increased by more than 2,000 percent since the end of the Second World War, very little of that increase has benefitted South Africa's black majority. Most of the black population continues to subsist below the poverty line.[6] In 1975, when the officially recognized absolute minimum for a black family of six was set at $127.65 per month, the *Financial Mail* reported that 63.5 percent of the black households earned monthly incomes of less than $92.[7] In 1976, South African blacks, who constitute 71 percent of the population, took home only 23 percent of the national income. The white 16 percent took home 67 percent of the earned wealth.[8] Although black per capita income is increasing, the high rate of inflation has contributed to a decline in real income for many black families. The increase in white income, on the other hand, has largely exceeded the pace of inflation. Consequently, during this period of tremendous economic growth, the ratio of white to black per capita income has increased, rather than diminished. The white to black per capita income ratio was 16 to 1 in 1966; it reached 17 to 1 in 1975.[9] In 1978, white workers were still paid an average of 5 to 20 times more than black workers.[10]

Intensification of Government Repression

Just as the benefits of economic growth have not "trickled down" to the black population, the projected increase in social and political rights has also failed to materialize. In fact, economic abundance has been accompanied by an intensification of political repression. Thousands of blacks have been imprisoned under an increasing number of South African security laws—statutes so comprehen-

6

sive that activities likely "to endanger the maintenance of law and order" can be construed as terrorism and punished by prison or death.[11] Between 1950 and 1978, more than 1,300 people were banned by the Minister of Justice.[12] A "banned" person may not belong to certain organizations, attend meetings or social gatherings, speak publicly, or be quoted in print. In 1976 alone, more than 40 banning orders were served, many of them

GROSS DOMESTIC PRODUCT 1946-1970

R Millions

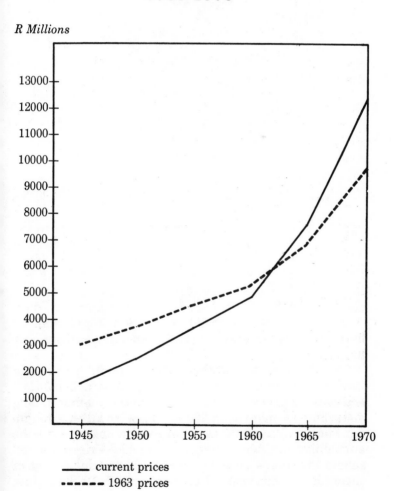

_____ current prices

------- 1963 prices

RACIAL COMPOSITION OF THE SOUTH AFRICAN POPULATION

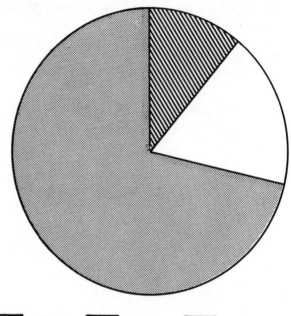

■ = Black ☐ = White ▨ = Asian & Colored

against trade unionists, journalists, and activists in the growing Black Consciousness Movement.[13] In a sweeping government clamp-down on October 19, 1977, 18 black organizations were banned, including the *World,* the largest black newspaper, and leading black organizations such as the Black People's Convention and the South African Students' Association (SASO). More than 50 black leaders were arrested and an unknown number banned.[14]

In the aftermath of the black township uprisings in 1976, the government's crack-down on black political activists increased markedly. During the six-month-long disturbances, more than 700 blacks were killed throughout South Africa. At least 85 of the victims were youths and children.[15] More than 1,000 blacks—including 150 school children—were detained without trial, many of them for over one year.[16] Between January 1976 and July

DISTRIBUTION OF NATIONAL INCOME ACCORDING TO RACE (1976)

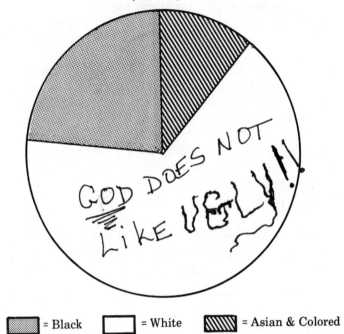

▨ = Black ☐ = White ▩ = Asian & Colored

1978, 26 political detainees died in police custody, including Black Consciousness leader, Steve Biko.[17]

For nearly a century, black South Africa resisted its government's racist laws through non-violent organizations. Black leaders have been banned, imprisoned, and murdered, their organizations outlawed. Throughout the 1950's, participants in the Defiance Campaigns against unjust laws were brutally beaten and imprisoned by the South African police. Sixty-nine black protestors died in the bloody massacre at Sharpeville in 1960, and 180 were wounded when South African police fired on a crowd of unarmed blacks. The African National Congress (ANC) and the Pan-Africanist Congress (PAC), the two leading black political organizations, were subsequently banned and their leaders imprisoned or forced to flee. The massacre at Sharpeville and the events that followed convinced the ANC and the PAC that armed struggle is

9

necessary for national liberation.

Sharpeville marked a turning point for the South African government as well. The regime's military expenditures multiplied rapidly after 1960—increasing over 600 percent in ten years' time. By 1977/78, the budget had again quadrupled, amounting to a total of $1.6 billion. In 1978/79, the budget had grown to $1.9 billion, and by 1979/80, it surpassed $2 billion. The dramatic increase in defense expenditures stimulated a new influx of foreign capital into the South African economy.[18] The white minority regime was interested in bolstering its security system with sophisticated new trucks, tanks, computers, and electronic equipment. Foreign companies rushed to meet the demand. Rather than discouraging foreign investment, the repressive South African military apparatus was actually encouraging it.

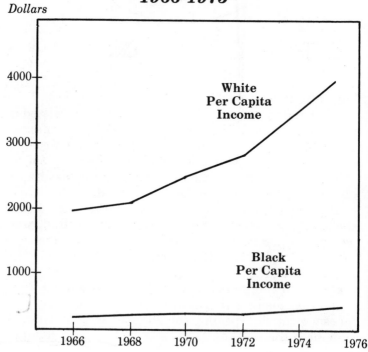

WHITE AND BLACK PER CAPITA INCOMES 1966-1975

The funeral of 13-year-old Hector Petersen, the first victim of police violence in the 1976 Soweto uprisings.
Peter Magubane

Polishing the Corporate Image

By the mid-1970's, in the face of unabated black poverty and rising political repression, American businesses were in a difficult position. They could present little proof of their positive impact on South Africa's black population. They provided jobs, but very few. Primarily capital-intensive, American companies employed less than one percent of the black workforce in South Africa.[19] While some of their black employees were being trained for skilled positions, only a small minority rose above the lowest job categories. The majority received wages that were far less than the pay whites received for comparable work. At the same time, American companies controlled

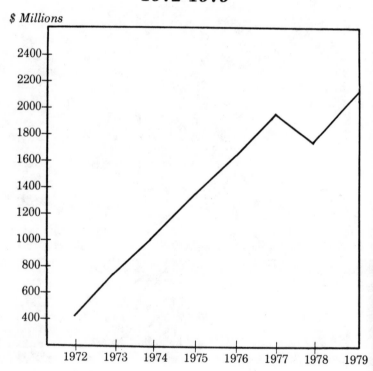

SOUTH AFRICAN DEFENSE EXPENDITURES 1972-1979

$ Millions

the most vital sectors of the South African economy, contributing capital, technological innovation, and expertise to the maintenance and expansion of the apartheid system. They had helped to create an economy based on the exploitation of cheap black labor, an economy controlled by a white minority that maintained a standard of living higher than almost any other population group in the world. None of the justifications of the business establishment could alter the fact that the real beneficiaries of American corporate involvement were South Africa's white minority, and of course, the corporations themselves.

An obvious boon to apartheid, American businesses had to make a concerted effort to change their image. They needed a concrete program of reform, in which progress could be measured and goals achieved. They needed *proof* that American companies could serve as a positive influence in South Africa and support for their argument that corporate withdrawal would only hurt the black population. The reformist scheme was not long in coming. By late 1975, there was muted talk of a new employment code for American companies doing business in South Africa. If they promised to adhere to certain employment practices, U.S. companies could mollify their critics at home and continue to do a profitable business in South Africa.

CHAPTER I
THE SULLIVAN PRINCIPLES: A CODE FOR CORPORATE REFORM

The pressures to get out of South Africa, coming from student and church quarters in particular, are staggeringly strong. And from what I can see, there is only one stumbling block to the dominance of this point of view. That stumbling block is the Rev. Leon Sullivan.
John Marquard, **The Johannesburg Star,**
March 31, 1979

In early 1977, the American business code of conduct was publicly introduced. Conceptualized by Reverend Leon H. Sullivan, a black civil rights activist and board member of General Motors, the six "Sullivan Principles" called for desegregation of the workplace, fair employment practices, equal pay for equal work, job training and advancement, and improvement in the quality of workers' lives. The principles were heralded by American business and government leaders as a positive step towards change—a peaceful, non-disruptive solution to the South African problem.

In actuality, the Sullivan Principles were a compromise solution. They were born out of a civil rights leader's frustrated attempts to reform the corporate world from the inside out. When Leon Sullivan was elected to the board of General Motors in 1971, he had been a prominent civil rights activist for more than a decade. He had organized massive boycotts of discriminatory Philadelphia businesses. He had established community-based manpower training programs that had prepared hundreds of thousands of minorities for skilled work. His successful programs were subsequently marketed throughout the world. When General Motors asked him to join their Board of Directors, Reverend Sullivan seized the opportunity to take his expertise and his anger into the corporate board room.

At his first board meeting, Leon Sullivan challenged the corporation to withdraw its business from South Africa. He declared that American businesses could not morally continue to function in "a country that so blatantly and ruthlessly and clearly maintains such dehumanizing practices against such large numbers of its people." He condemned the give-them-time attitude of his opponents "who always want to go slow when the rights of black men are at stake." Sullivan went on record as a proponent of corporate withdrawal:

> *I will continue to pursue my desire to see that American enterprises, including General Motors, withdraw from the Union of South Africa (sic) until clear changes have been made in the practices, the policies of that government as they pertain to blacks and other nonwhites . . .*

Although he realized his position would lose in 1971, Sullivan vowed that he would "continue to pursue it tomorrow until black people in the Union of South Africa are free."[20]

Within four years' time, however, Reverend Sullivan had changed his mind. Unable to convince a single colleague to support the withdrawal option and frustrated by the criticism that he was doing nothing to stimulate change, Sullivan opted for a more moderate plan—a code of conduct for American companies doing business in South Africa. In March 1977, after 18 months of hard campaigning, Reverend Sullivan announced the formulation of an employment code, endorsed by 12 of approximately 350 American businesses in South Africa. The six criteria for fair employment practices were immediately dubbed "the Sullivan Principles."

The Sullivan code caught on. In the wake of the Soweto uprisings and the rapid expansion of the divest-

Statement of Principles of U.S. Firms With Affiliates in the Republic of South Africa

Each of the firms endorsing the Statement of Principles have affiliates in the Republic of South Africa and support the following operating principles:

1. Non-segregation of the races in all eating, comfort and work facilities.

2. Equal and fair employment practices for all employees.

3. Equal pay for all employees doing equal or comparable work for the same period of time.

4. Initiation of and development of training programs that will prepare, in substantial numbers, Blacks and other non-whites for supervisory, administrative, clerical and technical jobs.

5. Increasing the number of Blacks and other non-whites in management and supervisory positions.

6. Improving the quality of employees' lives outside the work environment in such areas as housing, transportation, schooling, recreation and health facilities.

We agree to further implement these principles. Where implementation requires a modification of existing South African working conditions, we will seek such modification through appropriate channels.

We believe that the implementation of the foregoing principles is consistent with respect for human dignity and will contribute greatly to the general economic welfare of all the people of the Republic of South Africa.

ment movement in the United States, American business-men had grown apprehensive about the safety of their investments in South Africa. By the end of 1978, there were 105 signatories to the Sullivan Principles. One year later, there were 135.* The Sullivan plan for fair employment practices received nothing but praise from official circles. Written in consultation with U.S. business leaders, the Principles were hailed by the State Department "as a potentially major force for change in South Africa" and given the "strong support" of the United States government.[21] Challenged by the growing divestment movement, 75 colleges and universities, along with several trade unions, promoted the Sullivan Principles in their investment programs, stating that they would not divest their holdings in corporations that had signed them. Not even the South African government protested the implementation of the fair employment code.

By April 1979, however, prominent Americans had begun to criticize the Sullivan Principles. Two hundred black religious leaders met in New York to discuss American policy in South Africa. During the course of the three day conference, the churchmen overwhelmingly rejected the Sullivan Principles as a means of combatting apartheid. In a strongly worded resolution, they criticized the principles as "well-intentioned (but) no longer suffi-cient," claiming "that the very presence of United States corporations in South Africa serves to legitimize the apartheid system of white supremacy." The ministers then resolved "to work towards total United States economic, political, military, cultural and diplomatic disengagement from South Africa," and declared their "unequivocal support of the national liberation struggle waged by the South African people under the leadership of the African National Congress."[22]*

The resolution of the black churchmen was of para-mount importance. Many of these ministers had been civil rights activists since the early days of boycotts, strikes, and massive sit-ins. For nearly two decades, Reverend Leon H. Sullivan had been a leader among them. Now, the

*See Appendix I for a current list of signatory companies.
*See Appendix II for complete text of the resolution.

" 'Wait and see' is the watchword of the Sullivan Principles. 'Wait and see' in our American experience is a cruel hoax."

man who had decried gradualist reforms eight years before was being tried on the same charges. "My brother Leon Sullivan has a plan," thundered the Reverend Wyatt Tee Walker. "So have I!" He continued,

> *... Leon outlined six principles. I have but one! They are called the Sullivan Principles. My principle is not mine but God's principle. That principle is FREEDOM. Freedom of our South African brothers and sisters. Freedom of the children. Freedom of the land. Freedom of the ballot. Freedom from fear. Freedom from oppression. Freedom from hunger. Freedom, Freedom, Freedom!*
>
> *'Wait and see' is the watchword of the Sullivan Principles. 'Wait and see' in our American experience is a cruel hoax.*[23]

Monitoring the Sullivan Principles: The Cosmetics of Corporate Change

While Sullivan's critics condemned his reformist approach to apartheid, the employment code continued to gain support in the government, business, and corporate-investment communities. The International Council for Equality of Opportunity Principles was established by Reverend Sullivan to report on the progress of the signatory companies. The Arthur D. Little Company, a prestigious Cambridge research and consulting firm, was contracted to write progress questionnaires and compile them into summary reports, to be distributed to the public for a minimal fee. Reverend Sullivan held press briefings on the progress of the principles and hosted an official State Department dinner to honor the corporate signatories. Corporate executives, who at one time accused Sullivan of treading on their toes, praised the principles and lauded the efforts of the man who had written them.[24]

To date, the signatory companies have monitored their own compliance to the Sullivan Principles, filling out progress questionnaires twice a year. Theoretically, completion of the questionnaires is obligatory. However, there are no penalties for non-cooperation or for non-compliance with the employment principles. Nearly half of the signatories failed to respond to the first compliance questionnaire, and nearly one-fifth did not return the second and third questionnaires. Of those companies that responded, many left the most sensitive questions unanswered. One Ford Motor Company official admitted that many signatories "pay only lip service to the employment code," while another executive explained, "You have to remember who signed the principles. We didn't sign the principles, the home office did."[25] The *Citizen,* a Johannesburg newspaper, founded and financed by the South African government, dismissed the code as just another "universal code of conduct for the American pursuit of profits."[26]

Three compliance reports have been published since the initiation of the employment code. The first was released in November 1978, the second in April 1979, and the third in October 1979. The format of the reports has varied widely, rendering any long-term monitoring and evaluation of progress virtually impossible. Respondents to the first questionnaire were all considered to be "cooperative," simply because they participated in the reporting process. Non-respondents were not identified. The second report divided the companies into four categories:

I. Making Acceptable Progress
II. Cooperating
III. Non-Respondents
IV. Endorsers (with no operations in South Africa)

The vast majority of the respondents to the second questionnaire (66 out of 81) were considered to be "Making Acceptable Progress" in their implementation of the Sullivan Principles. In order to qualify for the top category, signatories had to: a) submit the first and second questionnaires; b) complete the desegregation of   19 their facilities (Principle #1) or show that they are "committed to major facility modifications to enable desegregation"; and c) show a "substantial commitment to implement the other principles." The second compliance report does not define "major facility modifications," nor require a definite schedule for their completion. Neither does the report indicate what criteria are used to determine whether or not a company's commitment to implementing the principles is "substantial."

The third compliance report ranked the companies on the basis of an elaborate point system. Those companies receiving 11 points or less were considered to be "Making Good Progress." Those who scored between 12 and 18 were judged to be "Making Acceptable Progress"; and those companies receiving more than 18 points "Need(ed) to Become More Active." None of the companies received nine, the perfect score. The majority of the respondents (62 out of 97) were again considered to be "Making Acceptable Progress" in their implementation of the Sullivan Principles.*

The third compliance report notes that "the criteria (for rating a company's performance) cannot be applied mechanically or in a specifically quantified way." Rather, the standards "must be applied with judgment."[27] Consequently, the evaluation of a company's performance is a subjective and somewhat arbitrary process.

According to the stipulations of the second and third compliance questionnaires, all signatories must file separate reports for each subsidiary location employing 50 workers or more. Ninety-seven signatories responded to the third compliance questionnaire, accounting for the practices of 244 separate subsidiary locations in South Africa. The majority of these companies are capital-intensive businesses employing a disproportionate number of skilled (white) workers. Although blacks comprise

---

*Other categories include:
IV. Inadequate Report
V. Submitting First Report
VI. Endorsers
VII. New Signatories (Joined too late to report)
VIII. Signatories Who Did Not Report
IX. Signatories Headquartered Outside the U.S.

72 percent of the labor force in South Africa, they comprise only 38 percent of the workforce in the companies that responded to the third compliance questionnaire. Whites, on the other hand, comprise only 18 percent of the nationwide labor force, but constitute 43 percent of the respondents' workplace population. Only 0.2 percent of South Africa's black workers are employed by the responding Sullivan signatory companies. These businesses employ approximately 31,000 blacks, coloreds, and Asians, from a non-white population of more than 22 million.

The impact of the Sullivan reforms must be considered within this limited context. Such progress that occurs affects only a minute fraction of South Africa's non-white population. The following analysis assesses the achievements of the signatory companies more than two and one-half years after the initiation of the Sullivan fair employment code.*

Decoding Corporate Camouflage

Principle # 1
Non-segregation of the races in all eating, comfort and work facilities.

Even within the limited scope of the signatory workplaces, change is occurring at a sluggish pace. According to the October 1979 compliance report, 75 percent of the 244 business locations claim that their facilities are now "common." This assertion is extremely misleading. While the companies may no longer post signs that segregate their facilities according to race, in point of fact, the majority of the facilities are *still* segregated. Information supplied under Principle #3 shows that 71 percent of the black workers still work in segregated workplaces—not because they are black, but because they perform the most menial or semi-skilled functions. Nearly three-quarters of the black workers are employed in job categories where there is not a single white worker.

---

*Unless otherwise indicated, all data has been obtained or extrapolated from the *Third Report on the Signatory Companies to the Sullivan Principles*.

RACIAL BREAKDOWN OF
THE SOUTH AFRICAN WORKFORCE

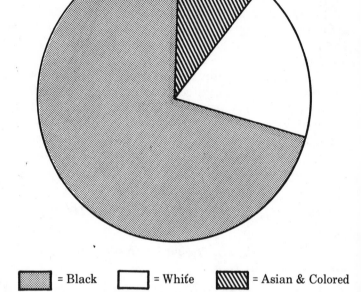

▨ = Black ☐ = White ▨ = Asian & Colored

Although the maintenance of workplace segregation has occurred fairly "naturally," a number of companies have made a conscious effort to ensure the continued segregation of eating and comfort facilities. After the exposure of General Motors' practice of substituting color-keyed for racially discriminatory signs—blue for whites, orange for blacks and coloreds—a subtler means of discrimination evolved. Technically in compliance with Principle #1, a number of companies have carefully removed the discriminatory signs from bathroom and cafeteria doors. Instead, lunchrooms, toilets, and locker-rooms that were previously assigned to black workers are now assigned to hourly workers; those previously reserved for white workers are set aside for salaried staff. In effect, the system of discrimination on the basis of race has been perpetuated.[28]

RACIAL BREAKDOWN OF THE WORKFORCE IN SULLIVAN SIGNATORY COMPANIES (1979)

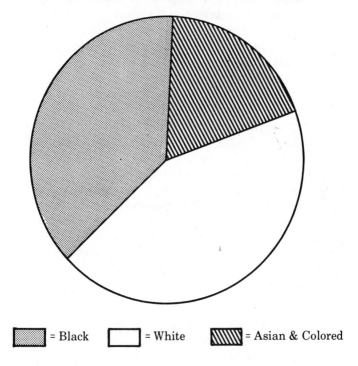

▨ = Black   ☐ = White   ◧ = Asian & Colored

Principle #2
Equal and fair employment practices for all employees.

When the Sullivan Principles were first introduced, they failed to include any mention of trade union rights. That omission caused such dissension from American critics that Reverend Sullivan was forced to include a trade union clause in the "Amplified Guidelines" of July 1978.* The result was an extremely ambiguous and comfortably noncommittal statement:

Each signator of the Sullivan Principles will proceed immediately to support the elimination of discrimi-

---

*See Appendix IV for most recent amplification of guidelines.

nation against the rights of Blacks to form or belong to government registered unions, and acknowledge generally the right of Black workers to form their own union or be represented by trade unions where unions already exist.

While the statement encourages the signatories to "support" the elimination of discrimination against black trade unions and to "acknowledge generally" the right of blacks to join or form their own trade unions, it does not require the companies to recognize black and white unions on an equal basis. It assumes that "government registered unions" will be free collective bargaining units, providing black workers with access to the same jobs and employment benefits as their white counterparts. Nothing in the history of South African labor relations substantiates that assumption.

As late as October 1979, 84 percent of the respondents to the Sullivan compliance questionnaire did not negoti-

24

ate with *any* employee union—white or black. Only two companies, Ford and Kellogg, had recognized black trade unions, and only Kellogg had actually signed a contract. However, even if all the signatories were to recognize black trade unions, unless those unions are legally registered, members have no protection under South African law. Their contracts are not binding; they have no recourse if the agreements are broken.

Even registered trade unions are severely hampered by legal restrictions. Although work slow-downs, strikes, and lock-outs are not absolutely banned, they are subject to so many restraints that a legal strike is practically impossible. In a number of "key industries," work-related protest is completely prohibited, and in any industry, going out on strike is a risky proposition. Strikers can be arrested under the *Internal Security Amendment Act of 1976* and charged with "communism," which in South Africa is defined as:

> . . . *any doctrine that aims at bringing about any political, industrial, social or economic change within the Union by the promotion of disturbance or disorder* . .

Dozens of trade unions and trade union organizers have been banned under this law. The *Riotous Assemblies Act* empowers local magistrates to prohibit public or private gatherings, concourses, or processions which they consider a threat to public order. Countless picketers have been arrested under this act. The *General Law Amendment Act (The Sabotage Act) of 1962,* the most blatant of South Africa's anti-strike laws, defines "sabotage" as any willful act threatening the maintenance of law and order and any attempt

> . . . *to cripple or seriously prejudice any industry, to cause substantial financial loss to any person or state, (or) to further or encourage the achievement of any political aim,* <u>*including bringing about social or economic change*</u> *(emphasis added).*

Sabotage is punishable as treason under South African law. The penalty could be death.

All workers, whether or not they are employed by 25

Sullivan signatories, are ultimately answerable to South African law. Until September 1979, when the South African government agreed to recognize *some* black trade unions, American corporations often pleaded that, because black unions were not legally recognized, their hands were tied. However, when the government announced the reform of its trade union laws, these same businesses were supplied with new ammunition for their argument that they constituted a "progressive force." They claimed that American companies could now provide a forum for black trade union development, helping the government along the road to reform. The government reforms, however, are far from progressive.*

Under the new regulations, recommended by the government-sponsored Wiehahn Commission, black workers from the urban areas, African homelands, and the so-called "independent" homelands are permitted to join registered trade unions. Migrant workers from Lesotho, Botswana, Swaziland, Mozambique, Malawi, and Zimbabwe—whose numbers are estimated at half a million—are still denied trade union rights.[29] The new black unions are being subjected to a stringent and arbitrary registration process that allows the government to deny or revoke registration at will. Government ministers have acknowledged that the primary purpose of the reforms is to bring militant black unions under strict government control, weeding out all politically "threatening" organizations.[30] Since the passage of the new labor legislation, an increasing number of companies have refused to deal with unregistered independent unions.

Principle #3
Equal pay for all employees doing equal or comparable work for the same period of time.

To the great majority of black workers who have been prevented from doing work that is "equal" to that of whites, "equal pay for equal work" is simply an empty slogan. According to the third compliance report, 76

*See "Afterword" for discussion of labor reforms proposed by the South African government's Wiehahn Commission.

To the great majority of black workers who have been prevented from doing work that is "equal" to that of whites, "equal pay for equal work" is simply an empty slogan.

percent of the workers in the lowest job category are black; two percent are white. Ninety-nine percent of the workers employed in the top job category are white; one percent is black. Twenty-two percent of the black workforce is employed in the lowest category of work. Seventy-one percent of the black workers in the signatory companies work in job categories that employ no whites. Only 10 percent of the black workers are employed in integrated job categories—*and* are earning at least the average income for their particular category.

The wage statistics of the Sullivan signatories are extremely grim. At the end of 1978, 95 percent of the companies that responded to the first questionnaire paid their entry-level workers less than $240 per month—$20 per month less than the Minimum Effective Level for Johannesburg. (The MEL is an official standard determined by the monthly cost of food, clothing, shelter, transportation, fuel, and medical and educational expenses for a family of six.) Nearly half of the black workers in the responding companies earned less than $175 per month, while half of the white workers earned at *least* $500 per month. International Harvester and Masonite were among the signatory companies that recorded starting wages that were below the Minimum *Subsistence* Level.[31]

Throughout South Africa, black wages have risen in recent years. However, the actual gap between black and white incomes has widened. In 1975, the gap between black and white wages averaged $447 per month in manufacturing and $665 per month in mining and quarrying. By 1979, the gap had widened to $665 and $880 per month respectively.[32] Since blacks begin working with wages that are much lower than those of whites, across-the-board wage increases accelerate, rather than alleviate, the growing income disparities. Last hired, first fired,   27 black workers will never achieve job seniority equal to that of whites.[33]

In a number of cases, the black/white wage differential is a product of legally binding Industrial Council Agreements. For years, these contracts between white workers and their employers have prevented companies from promoting blacks into thousands of skilled positions, including jobs that allow them to supervise whites. The severe shortage of skilled labor has forced a number of employers to strike a deal with the white unions; in exchange for softening some of the job restrictions, the employers promise white workers a disproportionate

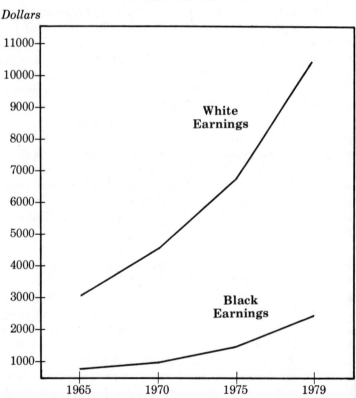

MANUFACTURING
AVERAGE EARNINGS PER ANNUM
FOR WHITE AND BLACK WORKERS
1965-1979

increase in wages.

"Job fragmentation" is another technique that enables companies to promote blacks into skilled positions without substantially increasing their wages. When white workers are promoted, their old jobs are watered down and redefined. Two or more blacks are hired to fill the positions for significantly less pay. The third compliance report does not indicate the average pay

MINING AND QUARRYING AVERAGE EARNINGS PER ANNUM FOR WHITE AND BLACK WORKERS 1965-1979

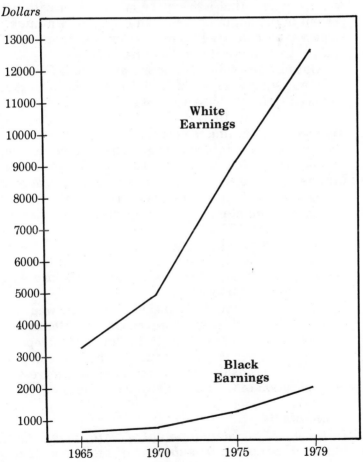

scales for black and white workers; nor does it show the racial composition of various grades of work within a given job category. Consequently, it is impossible to determine the amount of job fragmentation that has occurred within the signatory workplaces.

Historically, American corporations, including the Sullivan signatories, have employed very few blacks in salaried positions. In 1978, Goodyear employed a total of nine black salaried workers, comprising a mere three percent of its total white collar workforce. Uniroyal had no blacks in any salaried position at the end of 1978. In 1979, Ford employed 36 black salaried workers in a black workforce of 1,242. Forty-two percent of the black workers received wages that were at the minimum or within 10 percent of the minimum wage. In 1979, Ford's minimum wage was set at a rate 16 percent below the recommended MEL of the University of Port Elizabeth.[34]

Out of 1,184 salaried workers at General Motors in 1979, only eight were black. A total of three black workers had been added to the salaried staff at General Motors in three years' time. In 1979, more than half of the black workers were earning wages that were at or within 10 percent of the minimum wage. The minimum wage established by General Motors was 16 percent below the MEL recommended by the University of Port Elizabeth.[35]

A large portion of the labor force at the Masonite Corporation plantation sites is composed of unskilled black labor. In 1979, 240 of these workers were migrants who lived in single-sex hostels on the plantations. Nearly 40 percent of the black workforce on the plantations cut and stripped eucalyptus trees six days a week for a wage of $40 to $44 per month.[36]

In spite of these grave inequities in their wage and salary scales, Goodyear, Uniroyal, General Motors, and Masonite are all considered to be "making acceptable progress" in their implementation of the Sullivan Principles. Ford is considered to be "making good progress" in its application of the fair employment code.

Principle #4
Initiation of and development of training programs that will prepare, in substantial numbers, blacks

and other non-whites for supervisory, administrative, clerical and technical jobs.

In October 1979, one-fifth of the reporting companies had no occupational training programs. Overall, a slightly greater number of whites were being trained than blacks, although white workers already dominated the skilled labor force. Half of the blacks operated machines. By far the greatest number of blacks were *still* being trained as operators, rather than technicians, artisans, supervisors, or managers—effectively guaranteeing that the majority of the black workforce will remain in the lowest category of skilled work.

Corporate failure to train blacks for skilled positions can be explained, in part, by the strictures of South African law. According to a Firestone official, whose company is supposedly "making acceptable progress," it is pointless to train blacks as artisans because blacks are ineligible for certificates of competency, without which they cannot be employed. According to the Arthur D. Little Company, the consulting firm that writes and compiles the compliance questionnaires, highly skilled black craftsmen, who would otherwise qualify for artisan trade certificates, are often employed as "artisan apprentices," or "artisan trainees." However, since they lack job titles and descriptions equivalent to those of their white counterparts, Arthur D. Little consultant Ellen Ruppert added, "I would have the suspicion that they do not have the same pay."[37] The signatory companies were *not* asked to provide information concerning these potentially large pay differentials.

Closed shop agreements between white unions and their employers have also barred blacks from skilled work. Such agreements have reserved thousands of skilled positions for members of white trade unions. These unions, along with representatives of industry, control all apprenticeship programs. To date, these programs have not been open to blacks. Because the trade union reforms adopted in September 1979 will continue the tradition of racially segregated unions, blacks will be excluded from membership in those unions that now control the distribution of skilled positions. The new labor laws will perpetuate white monopolization of the skilled labor force. 31

White trade union opposition constitutes a major obstacle to the employment of blacks in skilled positions. The implementation of even the most limited workplace reforms has stimulated a tremendous white backlash. White workers have accused blacks of "dirtying" newly-integrated cafeterias and toilets. They have walked off their jobs in protest of black promotions and wage increases. Without the cooperation of the white workers and their unions, corporations can do very little to alter traditional hiring patterns. While relatively few jobs are

RACIAL COMPOSITION OF THE MANAGERIAL WORKFORCE IN SULLIVAN SIGNATORY COMPANIES (October 1979)

Percent

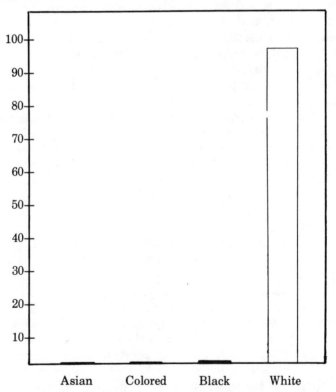

Note: Work-Study Trainees are included in the calculations for the trainee, rather than the managerial, population.

reserved for whites by law, tens of thousands are set aside by Industrial Council Agreements. Prospects for white union cooperation are grim. In a public statement, Arrie Paulus, General Secretary of the powerful white Mine Workers' Union, declared, "As far as my union is concerned his (the black man's) future is that of a laborer."[38] By skirting the legal and trade union obstacles, the Sullivan compliance report drastically misrepresents the potential for change in the black employment situation.

FUTURE COMPOSITION OF THE MANAGERIAL WORKFORCE IF ALL CURRENT TRAINEES ARE EMPLOYED

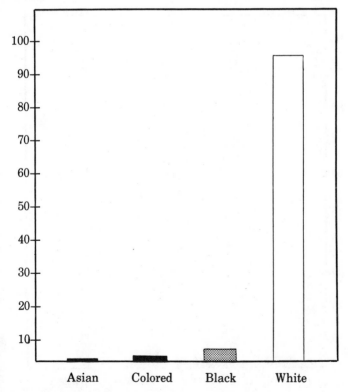

Percent

Note: Work-Study Trainees are included in the calculations for the trainee, rather than the managerial, population.

The compliance report is also misleading in its comparison of black and white benefits from the training programs. By choosing to report the number of black and white employees trained rather than the amount of money spent in training them, the compliance report obscures the discriminatory nature of company practices. The records of American computer companies are extremely revealing. All of the computer companies are either "making good progress" or "making acceptable progress"

RACIAL COMPOSITION OF THE PROFESSIONAL WORKFORCE IN SULLIVAN SIGNATORY COMPANIES (October 1979)

Percent

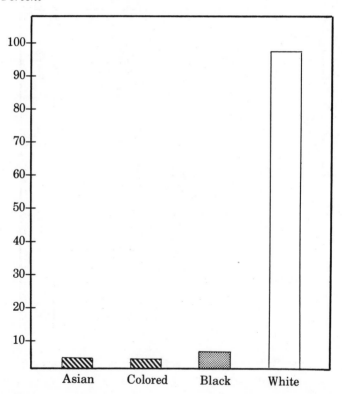

Note: Work-Study Trainees are included in the calculations for the trainee, rather than the professional, population.

in their implementation of the Sullivan Principles. Yet, blacks do not comprise more than 15 percent of the workforce in any American-owned computer company in South Africa. The companies recruit two to four times as many whites as blacks, and the majority of training funds are used to upgrade the skills of white workers. Most of the black trainees are enrolled in programs that teach clerical, rather than technical or managerial skills.[39] One computer company reported to the Investor Responsi-

FUTURE COMPOSITION OF THE PROFESSIONAL WORKFORCE IF ALL CURRENT TRAINEES ARE EMPLOYED

Percent

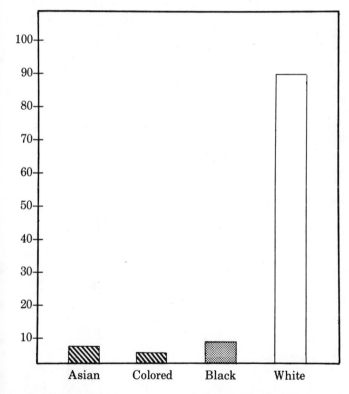

Note: Work-Study Trainees are included in the calculations for the trainee, rather than the professional, population.

bility Research Center that in 1978, it spent $67,000 on training for whites and only $3,300 on training for blacks.[40] The fact that these discriminating companies are in technical compliance with the Sullivan Principles is another indication of the code's ineffectuality.

RACIAL COMPOSITION OF THE ARTISAN WORKFORCE IN SULLIVAN SIGNATORY COMPANIES (October 1979)

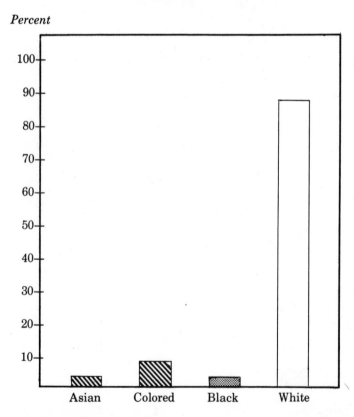

Percent

Note: Work-Study Trainees are included in the calculations for the trainee, rather than the artisan, population.

Principle #5
Increasing the number of blacks and other non-whites in management and supervisory positions.

Corporate compliance with the fifth Sullivan Principle has made very little advance. Nearly half of the respondents to the third compliance questionnaire employ no blacks in managerial or supervisory positions. Approximately one-third employ only whites in these job

FUTURE COMPOSITION OF THE ARTISAN WORKFORCE IF ALL CURRENT TRAINEES ARE EMPLOYED

Percent

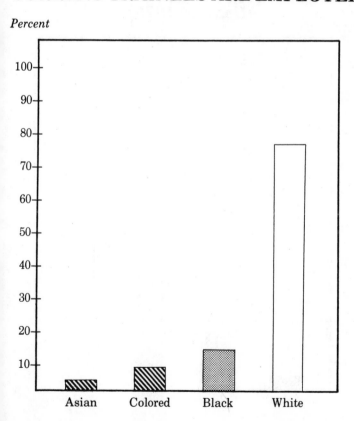

Note: Work-Study Trainees are included in the calculations for the trainee, rather than the artisan, population.

categories. A total of 43 black managers and 24 management trainees have been hired by the 97 signatories who responded to the third questionnaire—that is, 67 blacks out of a managerial staff of 3,243, employed in 244 separate workplaces.

Of the 21,029 blacks working in the reporting companies in October 1979, only 52 were being trained as managers and 103 as professionals. In other words, only 0.7 percent of the blacks working in signatory companies were involved in professional or managerial training pro-

RACIAL COMPOSITION OF THE WORKFORCE IN SULLIVAN SIGNATORY COMPANIES (October 1979)

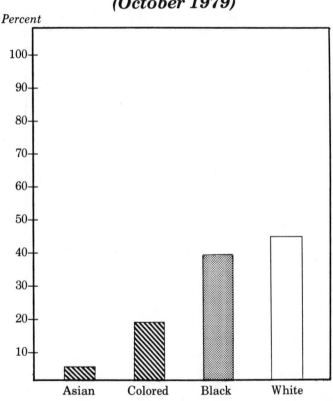

Percent

grams. Currently blacks constitute two percent of the managerial and four percent of the professional workforces; whites constitute 96 percent and 92 percent respectively. If all the trainees are hired when their programs are completed, blacks will still hold only three percent of the managerial and six percent of the professional positions. Whites will continue their virtual monopoly of these jobs by occupying 94 percent of the managerial and 89 percent of the professional slots. Since most of the

RACIAL COMPOSITION OF THE MANAGERIAL WORKFORCE IN SULLIVAN SIGNATORY COMPANIES (October 1979)

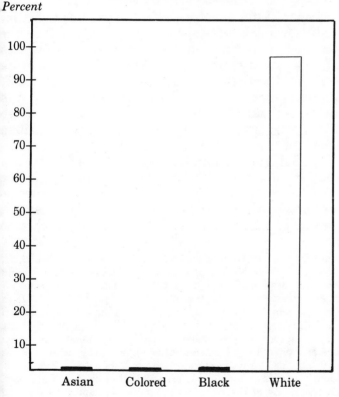

Percent

black workers are being trained for low-level positions and most of the whites for highly skilled work, the skewed ratio of white to black management, professional and skilled workers will remain constant.

According to the Arthur D. Little Company, managers are defined as "individuals who set broad policies, exercise responsibility for executing policies, or direct individual departments or components of a company's operations." Supervisors are persons who "supervise other individuals or an activity which is highly specific with respect to objectives and content, usually requiring specialized skills acquired on the job."[41] The third compliance report does not distinguish between various work grades within these broad categories. It does not differentiate between the managers who take charge of the companies' cafeteria facilities and those who oversee the companies' financial operations. According to Arthur D. Little consultant Ruppert, the 14 percent of the supervisory workforce who are black supervise whites "only in very, very rare cases." Black supervision of white workers is illegal in many industries, and, Ruppert stated, "The law in that respect is still quite strong." Ruppert was unable to estimate the number of blacks who *do* supervise white or integrated workforces since that particular item "was not measured."[42] *

The Sullivan compliance questionnaires failed to ask a number of other critical questions. As a result, the compliance report portrays the signatory companies as more "progressive" than they actually are. For example, one-third of the questionnaire respondents employ no

---

*According to a provision of the *Industrial Conciliation Act of 1924,* white workers and their employers may bar blacks from skilled and supervisory positions through Industrial Council Agreements. A number of industries have used this law to prevent blacks from supervising whites. For example, the building industry's Industrial Council Agreement states that if a black worker is promoted, white workers are to receive corresponding promotions, retaining their edge on skilled and supervisory positions. Although a number of signatories have disregarded various separate facilities laws without legal repercussions, supervisory regulations are enforced much more rigorously. Thus, the ability of the signatory companies to implement fair and racially unbiased employment practices is severely restricted by prejudicial South African laws.

non-whites in managerial/supervisory positions that are comparable to those held by whites. The Arthur D. Little report does *not* indicate how many companies employ no *blacks* in managerial/supervisory positions that are comparable to those held by whites. Given the traditional hiring patterns in South Africa, one can safely assume that the number would be even greater than one-third; the inclusion of hiring statistics for coloreds and Asians invariably skews the ratio downward. Similarly, the report does not indicate the relative *number* of whites and non-whites employed in "comparable positions." It makes no distinction between a company employing one black and 50 whites at comparable levels and one employing 29 blacks and 30 whites.

Finally, the Arthur D. Little Company defines "comparable position" in such broad terms that it seriously distorts the actual workplace situation. Any company that employs a white manager or supervisor and "also has one or more managers (or supervisors) of another race," is considered to have white and non-white managers/supervisors in comparable positions. Again, the report does not differentiate between the grades of work within each job category. To imply that all positions —and pay scales—are comparable is a total misrepresentation of the case.

A sampling of hiring practices in individual signatory companies illustrates the lack of progress on the fifth Sullivan Principle. As of June 1978, Union Carbide employed only white managers and supervisors. Three-quarters of the professional staff was also white. Exxon had no non-whites in management or professional positions. In June 1979, Ford Motor Company employed solely white managers. Ninety-five percent of Ford's professionals were white; four percent were black. Blacks comprised six percent of the supervisory workforce (whites, 72 percent); two percent of the artisans (whites, 89 percent); four percent of the technicians (whites, 89 percent); and nine percent of the clerical workers (whites, 47 percent). According to the third Sullivan compliance report, all of these companies are making either "good" or "acceptable" progress in their implementation of the equal employment code.[43]

41

Out of a total of 270 Control Data employees, ony 14 (5.2 percent) were black. . . . Nearly 73 percent of all white workers outranked the senior black employee.

The semblance of racial equality is not difficult to achieve if a corporation is capital-intensive and hires very few blacks. If only a handful of blacks are employed, the addition or promotion of one or two blacks translates into a much-improved percentage point record. Hewlett-Packard, for example, had a workforce of 79 in June 1978. Sixty-nine of those workers were white, and seven were black. According to the first Sullivan compliance questionnaire, Hewlett-Packard had no black managers or professionals, one black supervisor, two black artisans, and five black clerical workers.* One year later, the computer company was listed among those signatories who were "making good progress" in their implementation of the Sullivan Principles. If Hewlett-Packard added one black supervisor to its workforce between June 1978 and June 1979, its record in that category would have improved by 100 percent. If the company employed one black manager, its score would have soared over 100 percent in terms of employment practices improvement.

Control Data, like Hewlett-Packard, would be hard pressed to defend its employment record. In June 1979, the computer company employed a white workforce that was 16 times larger than the black workforce. Out of a total of 270 Control Data employees, only 14 (5.2 percent) were black. Although there are 10 categories of work in the company, all of the blacks were employed in the bottom three. Nine of the 14 blacks worked in the lowest job category. No blacks were being trained as sales personnel, technicians, supervisors, professionals, or managers. Nearly 73 percent of *all* white workers outranked the *senior* black employee.[44] In spite of its weak employment record, Control Data is considered to be "making good progress" in its implementation of the Sullivan fair employment principles.

*There was no explanation for the "extra" black position.

Honeywell has also been given a high rating by the Arthur D. Little Company. According to the third compliance report, Honeywell is "making acceptable progress" in its implementation of the Sullivan code. However, in June 1979, Honeywell employed 43 blacks in a workforce of 156. There were no blacks in managerial, supervisory, professional, artisan, technical, or sales positions. In 1979, only one black earned a salary at Honeywell. That employee was the only black who worked in a job category that also included white workers, and his salary did not even meet the average pay-level for the job category.[45] All white hourly workers were concentrated in the two highest pay grades, while Honeywell's black employees worked within the eight lowest grades of pay.[46]

Principle #6
Improving the quality of employees' lives outside the work environment in such areas as housing, transportation, schooling, recreation and health facilities.

The evaluation of signatory progress in the implementation of the sixth Sullivan Principle is severely lacking in detail. One of the two tables shows the numbers of blacks, whites, coloreds, and Asians benefitting from each type of assistance. It does *not* show the amount of money allotted to the employees in each racial group. Consequently, it is impossible to determine whether or not the benefits were evenly distributed, whether individuals were substantively assisted, or whether corporate efforts were no more than token gestures. While the table shows that blacks were the recipients in 55 percent of the instances of subsidized schooling, scholarship, and other educational assistance—it does *not* mean that they received 55 percent of the allocations. White children were the beneficiaries of 75 percent of the scholarships donated by corporate signatories. Black children received only 11 percent—in spite of the fact that the South African government spends 10 to 20 times more on each white student than on each black.[47]

According to the second compliance report, released in April 1979, housing aid fell at the bottom of the benefit

43

list. In 1978, the 177 reporting locations contributed a total of $23,777 towards employee housing—or 0.6 percent of their total assistance allocations. If the housing funds were evenly distributed, each of the 3,989 housing aid recipients would have received $5.96 to shelter his family for one year. However, given the characteristically unequal distribution of benefits in South Africa, it is more than likely that the white workers received a disproportionate amount of the benefits and that black families were given substantially less than $5.96 apiece.

By the time the third compliance report was released in October 1979, corporate contributions to employee housing had greatly improved. However, the 5,387 housing aid recipients still received a token amount of assistance. During the first half of 1979, they received an average of $91.68 per employee. At the same time there was a waiting list of nine years for rental accommodations in the townships. Blacks, who are now allowed to purchase homes—but not land—in the township areas, have been told that they will never find a house unless they buy one. The cheapest homes outside Johannesburg cost nearly $8,000 and require a downpayment of $1,840.[48] When nearly half of the black workers in signatory companies earned less than $2,100 per year in 1978, the prospect of purchasing such a home is virtually inconceivable. Within this context, signatory contributions for housing assistance are hardly significant.

Some signatory companies have made home improvement loans to black employees who already have living accommodations. Ford Motor Company, for example, granted a total of 29 home improvement loans to black workers between 1972 and 1978—that is, an average of five loans per year for a black employee population of 1,278.[49] According to a report by the Investor Responsibility Research Center, some signatories have refused to make home improvement loans to blacks because most of them do not own property, and thus have no collateral.[50]

While the 135 Sullivan signatory companies contributed less than $500,000 toward employee housing during the first six months of 1979, the black housing crisis has reached astronomical proportions. South African government sources estimate that 500,000 black homes are needed—but not planned—every year for the next two decades. Given the current state of affairs, $91.68 per employee—or less for blacks—can hardly be considered an "improve(ment) in the quality of employees' lives."

Paying Lip Service to Reform

In October 1979, more than two and one-half years after the Sullivan Principles were first introduced, the employment picture in signatory companies looked extremely bleak. Seventy-one percent of the black workers still worked in segregated job categories; nearly one-quarter were employed in the lowest category of work. Approximately one-half of the respondents to the third compliance questionnaire employed no blacks in managerial or supervisory positions. Only one company had signed a contract with a black trade union. Three-quarters of the scholarships distributed by the signatories went to white children. The amount of housing aid provided during the first six months of 1979—if evenly matched for the remaining six months and evenly distributed among the 5,387 recipients—would allow a black employee to purchase a home, only if he received an equal amount of money every year for 44 years.

If the Sullivan Principles are not working within the limited context of signatory workplaces, they will certainly not impact upon South Africa as a whole. If signatory companies will not implement progressive practices on their own factory floors, it is preposterous to think that they can serve as a "progressive force" in South Africa. While these companies provide jobs to only 0.2 percent of South Africa's black workers, they perform some of the most vital functions in the apartheid economy. They help to sustain a system that deprives 18.6 million black people of citizenship, political rights, and legal recourse. They provide critical support to a legal structure that denies nearly three-quarters of the population the right to own land, live with their families, move freely about the country, and work at jobs of their own choosing. Finally, they bolster an economy that denies the majority of the population a basic education, decent

45

housing, and adequate health care. While these companies make gestures toward reform, their changing labor practices do not portend the destruction of apartheid. The training of blacks for skilled work is simply a concession to the changing needs of the apartheid economy. The implementation of the Sullivan Principles is intended not to eliminate apartheid, but to "modernize" it and ensure its perpetuation.

The Sullivan signatories have failed to fulfill their stated purpose. Yet, the employment code has served the needs of its proponents. It has smoothed the path of American corporations who want to profit from the cheap labor economy without interference from dissatisfied black workers or a critical American public. It has served the interests of the United States government, allowing it to profess a progressive policy without actually confronting the white minority regime. Finally, the Sullivan code has benefitted the South African supporters of the apartheid system. It has allowed them to appear tolerant because they have not opposed the code's implementation. It has ensured the safety of American capital and technology, investments that strengthen and perpetuate the apartheid system.

The major group not served by the Sullivan employment code is the group of 22 million non-white South Africans—three-quarters of the country's people. The vast majority of these people have not benefitted from any degree of employment reform. To them, the Sullivan Principles mean business as usual—the continuation of American investments which bolster the apartheid economy. Whether or not the code is implemented is irrelevant to their lives. Such "improvements" upon the system will only prolong their suffering.

Moderate Reforms With Limited Scope

The Sullivan signatories have failed to bring about significant employment reform. They have touched the lives of a very limited number of people. Yet, the real weakness of the employment code lies not in its faulty implementation, but in its underlying intention. The purpose of the Sullivan Principles is reform, not radical change. The principles were never meant to strike at the root of apartheid. They make no demand for black political rights. They do not challenge the policy of separate development. They do not call for the abolition of forced migratory labor or the pass laws—the legal network that ensures white capital a controlled supply of cheap black labor. The Sullivan Principles ignore the fact that black impoverishment is the product of a legal structure that denies blacks the right to acquire skilled work and effectively organize to protect themselves as workers. They do not challenge the laws that prevent three-quarters of the population from owning land and conducting business throughout most of South Africa. The Sullivan Principles are piecemeal reforms that allow a cruel system to survive.

The American business code treats apartheid as a matter of unfair employment practices that can be remedied through the implementation of a corporate code of conduct. However, apartheid is *not* simply a matter of racial discrimination. It is an economic system, legitimized by law and enforced by a powerful police state. Its primary purpose is to concentrate the nation's wealth and power in the hands of the white minority. To discuss "affirmative action" hiring practices for blacks is an absurdity, in light of the fact that they constitute nearly three-quarters of the country's population. Black impoverishment is not incidental to the system. The creation of a vast reservoir of cheap powerless labor, through the economic dispossession of the majority of the South African population, is the foundation upon which the structure of apartheid is built. The Sullivan Principles do not address—much less challenge—these fundamental economic issues.

"The Sullivan Code Has Failed"— Opposition from Black South Africa

If the Sullivan Principles miss the point of apartheid, it was not through oversight. Reverend Sullivan wrote the principles in consultation with white South African business leaders; the final draft was approved by the

South African government. At no stage in the initial development were black workers or community leaders consulted. The South African government saw to it that any threatening words were removed and that the stipulated reforms were not too specific. One notable change concerned corporate intervention in South African affairs. The initial draft read:

Where the implementation (of the code) requires a modification of existing South African laws and customs, we will seek modification through appropriate channels.

At the request of the South African authorities, Sullivan deleted "laws and customs" from the final draft and wrote only of modifying "working conditions."

Reverend Sullivan now claims that he has consulted "black leaders living in South Africa" with regard to the employment code.[51] However, these channels of communication have only recently opened. It was not until July 1979 that the signatory companies established a monitoring committee which included black South African leaders. In December 1979, following the dismissal of 700 striking black workers at a Ford plant in Port Elizabeth, three of the most prominent members of the committee resigned. Percy Qoboza, former editor of the *World,* Dr. Nthato Motlana, chairman of the Soweto Committee of Ten, and Bishop Desmond Tutu, General Secretary of the South African Council of Churches, told the press that the Ford dispute indicated that "the Sullivan code has failed." Dr. Motlana was particularly disturbed by the silence with which Reverend Sullivan and his associates had greeted the dispute.[52]

Long before they joined the Sullivan Principles monitoring committee, Dr. Motlana and Bishop Tutu had been critics of international economic ties to South Africa. In April 1978, Motlana told the *New York Times:*

If I said that the only way to bring change would be total economic sanctions, I would be liable to go to jail. So let's just be cagey. Let's just say that I support 'pressures,' and leave it at that.[53]

48

In the fall of 1978, Bishop Tutu told the press:

We ask our friends to apply economic pressure . . . Our last chance for peaceful change lies in the international community applying political, diplomatic and especially economic pressure . . . Any black leader who calls for economic sanctions is already guilty of treason under the Terrorism Act and subject to five years in prison or death. We have said as much as we can possibly say. We hope we have reasonably intelligent friends overseas who will know what we're saying.[54]

According to Massachusetts Senator Paul Tsongas, who visited South Africa shortly after the resignations, the sentiments expressed by the three black leaders are the rule, rather than the exception in the black community. Tsongas reported that he met with at least 20 blacks, not one of whom was in favor of continued U.S. investment in South Africa—with or without the Sullivan Principles. Even those leaders who had promoted U.S. investment in the past are no longer advocating it, Tsongas said. These leaders have not publicly called for disinvestment because such statements are punishable as treason in South Africa.[55]

Although Reverend Sullivan may still find some support for his employment code among certain "black leaders living in South Africa," he will not find support in the exiled community. The national liberation movement has taken a strong position against any foreign investments in South Africa.* In November 1977, the African National Congress stated that:

The call for the international isolation of South Africa has come initially from the people of South Africa. No organization, save those that accept apartheid and work within the system, has supported continued foreign investment in the apartheid economy.[56]

The same year, John Gaetsewe, General Secretary of the

---

*See Appendix III for text of ANC statement regarding foreign investments.

49

***Even the South African government is
aware that apartheid's petty features
must be abolished in order to preserve
the foundation of the entire system.***

banned South African Congress of Trade Unions
(SACTU) declared that:

> *The ending of foreign investment in South Africa ... is
> a means of undermining the power of the apartheid
> regime. But it is of such importance that there can be no
> compromise whatsoever about it from our point of view.
> Foreign investment is a pillar of the whole system
> which maintains the virtual slavery of the Black
> workers in South Africa.*[57]

Many of the black leaders who had previously condemned
all forms of foreign investment were willing to give the
Sullivan Principles a chance. However, the massive
firings at Ford, followed by three prominent resignations
from the Sullivan monitoring committee, destroyed all
remnants of support for the code among leading black
South Africans.

Abiding by the Terms
of South African Law

If the South African government has not obstructed the
implementation of the Sullivan Principles, it is because
they do not threaten apartheid's basic structure. Only the
first principle entails a possible violation of South African
law; the desegregation of facilities is illegal in certain
types of businesses. While some signatory companies
have refused to integrate on the grounds that they would
be breaking their host country's laws, the South African
government has turned its back on such minor infractions
by other signatory companies. If it takes the integration
of lunchrooms and toilets to ensure the survival of a cheap
labor economy, then these token changes must be made. If
domestic pressure requires that American corporations
reform their employment practices or get out of South
Africa, the minority regime will allow them to implement

superficial employment reforms. Even the South African government is aware that apartheid's petty features must be abolished in order to preserve the foundation of the entire system.

Signatory companies have perceived it to be in their best interests to cooperate with the white minority regime. The South African government and its agencies are among their major business clients. To confront the apartheid system—and the cheap labor and high profits that it entails—would be antagonistic to their business senses. However, if these companies were pressed to challenge apartheid structures, any significant action would be blocked by South African law. Parent companies in the United States have no legal jurisdiction over the activities of their subsidiaries in South Africa. All companies operating in South Africa must comply with the terms of the *National Supplies Procurement Act,* which empowers the Minister of Economic Affairs to order any company to manufacture on demand any product the government determines to be essential to national security. If a company refuses to comply, the government "may, without legal process, seize the goods in question" or take over the company's production processes. When the law was activated in 1977, the *Financial Mail* wrote, "It is the general impression that foreign controlled firms supplying the Department of Defence could be commandeered if their parents instruct them to stop supplying goods which (the government) needs."[58]

After the black uprisings of 1976 and 1977, the South African government passed a number of laws prohibiting the release of "strategic" business information to foreign individuals, governments, or corporations. The *Atomic Energy Act of 1978* and the *Petroleum Products Act of 1977* prohibit the release of nuclear and energy-related information. The *Petroleum Products Act* authorizes the Minister of Economic Affairs to regulate the purchase, sale, or use of any petroleum product. Under South African law, oil companies must sell their products to any credit-worthy South African customer—including the South African security forces. The terms of the *Official Secrets Act* prohibit foreign subsidiaries from disclosing the details of energy-related agreements between the subsidiaries and the South African government. In fact, they are not even permitted to reveal whether or not these agreements exist. Any one of these statutes could prevent American subsidiaries from complying with a U.S. government order to report on their activities or to cease all sales of strategic materials to the South African government and its agencies.

South Africa has learned to cover its flanks. It can commandeer supplies. It can censor information. In the summer of 1978—largely in response to the introduction of the Sullivan compliance questionnaires—the government passed the *Protection of Business Act,* rendering it a criminal offense to pass *any* business-related information out of South Africa, unless granted permission to do so by the Minister of Economic Affairs. The express purpose of the Act is:

> *To restrict the enforcement in the Republic of certain foreign judgments, orders, directions, arbitration awards and letters of request; to prohibit the furnishing of information relating to businesses in compliance with foreign orders, directions, or letters of request; and to provide for matters connected therewith.*

Subsidiaries operating in South Africa can be prevented from giving information to their parent companies—even if ordered to do so by an American court. As a consequence of this act, *signatories to the Sullivan Principles must file their compliance questionnaires with the South African government before forwarding them on to the United States.* A number of companies, failing to give detailed accounts of their activities in South Africa, cited this law as their obstacle.[59]

The *Protection of Business Act* has even prevented the United States *government* from obtaining information concerning the activities of American subsidiaries in South Africa. One State Department official reported that, throughout his fact-finding tour of U.S. subsidiary operations, company executives consistently brought South African lawyers to their interviews. These lawyers would prompt the businessmen, telling them which questions they could not answer without breaking South

African law.[60] If parent companies cannot get the truth from their South African subsidiaries, and the United States government cannot obtain detailed reports on U.S. corporate activities under the apartheid system, how can American businesses guarantee their subsidiaries' compliance with the Sullivan Principles? Reverend Sullivan has declared that he would use his personal influence to counter the implementation of such laws as the *National Supplies Procurement Act.* Yet it is difficult to believe that his arguments could alter the government's strategic course.[61]

Monitoring the Monitors

It is our firmly considered view that liberal opinion—however well-intentioned it may appear—that opposes our campaign for (corporate) withdrawal is, in the long run, only delaying the change that is essential if South Africa is to be rid of apartheid and slave labor. It is not enough to grant higher wages here, better conditions there, for this leaves the apartheid system intact, in fact it props it up for longer—the very source of our misery and degradation.

African National Congress

The Edna McConnell Clark Foundation

Although American companies clearly have a stake in South Africa's present economic system, signatories to the Sullivan Principles have been asked to monitor their own compliance with the fair employment code. Outside of the companies' semi-annual compliance question-naires and the reports of the problem-ridden Sullivan monitoring committee in South Africa, there has been no way to gauge the progress of the Sullivan signatories.

In order to obtain a "non-corporate" perspective on the signatory companies' progress, Reverend Sullivan has initiated an on-site monitoring program. A group of three to five Americans, selected by the International Council for Equality of Opportunity Principles, is sched-uled to tour a number of signatory facilities in the summer of 1980. A small group of South Africans will also tour the plants. A general report will be written, 53 summarizing the data obtained from all of the companies. According to the International Council's executive director, Daniel Purnell, the report will be used for internal purposes and will not be available for public distribution.[62]

Although the purpose of the on-site monitoring program is purportedly to acquire an impartial view of the principles' implementation process, the program sponsor is itself deeply involved in South Africa. The Edna McConnell Clark Foundation, a New York-based philanthropic organization whose assets are valued at $199 million, has provided grants totalling $80,000 to cover the cost of the monitoring trip.[63] Ranked among the 20 largest foundations in the world, the Clark Foundation has more than $60 million—one-third of its total assets—invested in companies doing business in South Africa.[64]

In a statement released May 5, 1980, Edna McConnell Clark Foundation president, John R. Coleman, explained the foundation's motivations for giving the grant:

> *The suggestion that our support for monitoring the Sullivan signatories' actions is motivated in any way by our investments in companies doing some part of their business in South Africa is pure, unadulterated hogwash. I am the one who framed the recommendation for support and the one who sold our Trustees on it. Not once then, and not once since, did I assume we should do this to preserve our investments.*
>
> *Our support was solely because, believing that American corporations would do better to stay in South Africa and move as rapidly toward equal opportunity as possible, we felt someone should be there looking over their shoulders and prompting them to act. If the Sullivan Principles can produce proven progress without violence, that is enough for us in human terms, the only terms that influenced our grant.*

The Arthur D. Little Company

Prior to obtaining the grants from the Clark Foundation, the International Council supported its operations solely through personal and corporate gifts. At a press

54

conference in October 1979, Reverend Sullivan stated that much of the money came out of his own pocket, those of his fellow ministers, or was donated by the congregation of his 6,000 member Zion Baptist Church. Reverend Sullivan also stated that the signatory companies have borne some of the costs of running the International Council as well as the full expense of compiling the compliance questionnaires and reports.[65] A large portion of these expenses have been paid to the Arthur D. Little Company in Cambridge, Massachusetts for its analysis of the compliance data and its publication of the summary reports.

Working with apartheid is not new to the Arthur D. Little Company. Prior to its contract with Sullivan's International Council, the prestigious consulting firm had other business connections with South Africa. For more than a decade, Arthur D. Little has had economic and managerial links to the Space Research Corporation, a company whose top officials have pleaded guilty to illegally shipping arms to South Africa. In December 1978, the *Rutland Herald* reported that the Arthur D. Little Company had acquired 50 percent ownership of Space Research in the mid-1960's, in exchange for providing administrative and technical assistance to the financially ailing company. In September 1968, four Arthur D. Little executives joined the Space Research board. A few years later, the Arthur D. Little Company deeded its Space Research equity to its own majority holding company, a multi-million dollar investment trust fund, Memorial Drive Trust. According to Jean de Valpine, chief executive officer of Memorial Drive Trust, and chairman of the board of Space Research until 1977, the trust fund continued to be a major shareholder in the Space Research Corporation until 1978, the same year that a federal grand jury launched an investigation into the corporation's activities.[66]

In March 1980, the two chief officers of Space Research pleaded guilty to shipping some 53,000 extended-range artillery shells to South Africa—in violation of U.S. law, United Nations sanctions, State Department regulations, and the customs agreements of several countries. The pleas grew out of a 15-month-long federal grand jury investigation, which uncovered evidence that Space Research had shipped an estimated $50 million worth of artillery shells and technology from the United States to South Africa between 1976 and 1978, following a circuitous route that involved several countries.

A few days prior to the entrance of the guilty pleas, the *Burlington Free Press* revealed that Space Research has been one-fifth owned by the South African government since 1977. *Free Press* reporters Sam Hemingway and William Scott Malone established that, through a complex financial arrangement, the South African government was able to funnel $10 million into Space Research in 1977, acquiring 20 percent ownership and saving the company from economic bankruptcy.[67]

South Africa's search for sophisticated extended-range artillery shells began in October 1975. At that time, a South African military official approached the CIA station chief in Pretoria, requesting the extended-range 155mm howitzer shells for use against Cuban troops in Angola. Officially, the CIA denied the request. However, "unofficially," CIA operative, Colonel John J. Clancey, began scouting out a commercial supplier for the shells.[68]

According to John Stockwell, then head of the CIA's Angola Task Force, Clancey claimed that he had located a commercial supplier through an arms dealer in Belgium. The dealer, Colonel "Jack" Frost, had helped Clancey obtain arms for the CIA's $50 million covert operation in Angola and was listed in State Department documents as a consultant to Space Research during its earlier sale of howitzer shells to Israel.[69] At the suggestion of Jack Frost, five top South African military officers visited Space Research in early 1976. By April, representatives of the Space Research Corporation and the South African government had signed an agreement for the sale of 53,000 155mm shells through a Space Research affiliate in Belgium.[70]

The extent of U.S. government involvement in the illegal arms transaction has not yet been fully exposed. However, there is documented evidence that officials at various levels of the government were aware that a deal was being made. In late 1975, Jack Frost informed the Office of Munitions Control at the State Department that

As late as March 1978, at the same time that the Arthur D. Little Company was undertaking the task of monitoring corporate compliance to the Sullivan Principles, Space Research was involved in illegal arms sales to South Africa.

he had advised the South African military to contact the Space Research Corporation concerning a possible arms transaction. The State Department took no action to prevent the negotiations from going any further. In early May 1976, the Pentagon received a Space Research request to purchase 50,000 shell forgings (semi-finished shells) from an army munitions plant in Scranton, Pennsylvania. The sale was approved in record time, and Space Research was exempted from Defense Department regulations that require written indication of the shells' destination and purpose. At the same time, the Office of Munitions Control waived the requirement that Space Research obtain an export license to ship the forgings across the border into Canada, where the company's manufacturing facilities are located.[71] On three separate occasions between December 1977 and January 1978, U.S. Navy-chartered vessels shipped the finished shells from Port Canaveral, Florida, to Antigua, from whence they were shipped to South Africa.[72]

If the United States government was aware of an irregular arms transaction involving the Space Research Corporation, it is highly unlikely that the corporation's Board of Directors got no wind of it. At least 10 Space Research engineers and technicians took extended trips to South Africa in 1977 and 1978 to train South African military officers in the use of the new equipment. The leader of the Space Research team was later employed by one of the South Africa companies that received the artillery shells.[73] Throughout most of this period, Jean de Valpine was chairman of the board of the Space Research Corporation, indirectly representing the interests of the Arthur D. Little Company.

As late as March 1978, at the same time that the

57

Arthur D. Little Company was undertaking the task of monitoring corporate compliance to the Sullivan Principles, Space Research was involved in illegal arms sales to South Africa. Simultaneous with the promotion of the Sullivan plan for "ending apartheid ... without a violent war, and without the loss of untold numbers of lives," Space Research was assisting the apartheid regime in its efforts to arm a military devoted to defending apartheid by force.[74] An obvious conflict exists between the Arthur D. Little Company's involvement in the Space Research scandal, through the interests of its majority holding company, and its monitoring of the Sullivan equal employment code. In spite of these revelations, Reverend Sullivan has publicly avowed his faith in the judgment and competency of the firm and has made no inquiry into the issue.[75]

CHAPTER II
THE STRATEGIC ROLE
OF SULLIVAN
SIGNATORIES

NCR does not pretend that ending apartheid or changing other aspects of the South African society is our main reason for wanting to continue our operations in South Africa. Our primary purpose, as is true with other U.S. corporations, is to strengthen our company, for the good of our shareholders, and by extension to strengthen the U.S. economy as a whole. We believe this is a legitimate goal and one that should not be toyed with through political manipulation which is not likely to affect the desired result . . .

B. Lyle Shafer, Vice President, NCR
To the U.S. House of Representatives,
July 12, 1978

The signatories to the Sullivan Principles are among the U.S. corporations with the greatest stake in the South African system. They control the most strategic sectors of the economy—33 percent of the motor vehicle market, 44 percent of the petroleum products market, and 70 percent of the computer market. Even more important than American investment has been the transfer of American technology and expertise. According to British economist, John Suckling, the input of new technology and know-how has been *the* most important contribution of foreign investment to the South African economy—accounting for 40 percent of the growth in South Africa's GDP between 1957 and 1972. The most significant contribution has come from American companies, among them the most prominent signatories to the Sullivan Principles.[76]   59

According to a Senate Foreign Relations Committee report released in January 1978, American investments and loans have provided critical assistance to the South African government during the periods of its worst economic difficulties. That assistance will cushion the blow of any punitive actions against the regime by the world community:

International credit provided the margin of funds needed by South Africa in the 1974-76 period to finance its military buildup, its stockpiling of oil, and its major infrastructure projects in strategic economic sectors such as transportation, communications, energy, and steel production, all of which are related to security needs.*

* * *

The net effect of American investment has been to strengthen the economic and military self-sufficiency of South Africa's apartheid regime, undermining the fundamental goals and objectives of U.S. foreign policy.[77]

Although the strategic significance of American involvement in South Africa has been studied from a variety of perspectives, none of the studies have focused on the Sullivan signatories per se. These corporations are considered to be among the most progressive businesses in South Africa. Their implementation of "fair employment practices" has been heralded as the inspiration for a new business trend—the ending of apartheid on the factory floors. Unfortunately, the employment practices of Sullivan signatories do not vary greatly from those of non-signatory companies. There have been no real advances towards equal employment practices and equal pay. The Sullivan Principles are being used to camouflage

---

*South Africa's concern with military and strategic stockpiling has been growing steadily since the mid-1970's when national liberation forces overthrew the Portuguese colonialists in the neighboring countries of Angola and Mozambique, and black unrest in the urban townships broke to the surface in South Africa. The looming threat of international sanctions and the cut-off of Iranian oil in early 1979 dramatized the urgency of South Africa's program for strategic self-sufficiency.

corporate collaboration with apartheid. In this regard, signatories to the Sullivan Principles are among the worst offenders.

The Motor Vehicle Industry

The October 1979 Sullivan compliance report considers Ford Motor Company to be "making good progress" and General Motors to be "making acceptable progress" in their implementation of the Sullivan Principles. However, the contributions that these companies make to the apartheid government far outweigh their "good progress" in the implementation of the Sullivan Principles. Ford and General Motors provide the South African military and police establishments with motor vehicles, in spite of the 1978 Commerce Department regulations which prohibit the sale of *any* American commodity to the South African military or police. Ford and G.M. by-pass the regulations by providing these agencies with South African-made vehicles that do not contain any American-made component parts. Likewise, Firestone and Goodyear—also deemed to be "making acceptable progress"—sell tires to the South African government. These tires, which can be used on military or police vehicles, are made by American subsidiaries located outside the United States.

Even if the Commerce Department regulations were to be more rigorously worded and enforced, U.S. government precautions would have little effect. According to an American Committee on Africa report, 90 percent of all sales to the South African government pass through a central clearinghouse similar to the U.S. General Services Administration. Consequently, Ford, G.M., Firestone, and Goodyear could continue to fill the needs of the South African security forces by funneling all contracts through the central government.[78]

General Motors

While the motor vehicle industry undermines the intentions of American law, it has pledged absolute obedience to the law of South Africa. In response to an inquiry about the company's relationship to the South

61

African government, G.M. chairman Charles Murphy wrote,

> It is apparent to us that manufacturing plants involved in such basic industries as petroleum production and refining, mining primary metals, transportation, and machinery—industries which generate the lifeblood of any economy—also assume equally strategic importance in time of emergency. Any of our plants can be converted to war production as clearly demonstrated in the United States in 1941.[79]

What Chairman Murphy did *not* say is that General Motors has its own contingency plan to be implemented "in the event of civil unrest" or "national emergency"— i.e. black rebellion.[80]

According to the terms of the G.M. contingency plan, the company agrees to cooperate fully with the South African Ministry of Defense, which would establish "a military presence on the property," control "all aspects of security . . . regulate output and coordinate the entire industrial effort." G.M. states that it would act to "meet imposed requirements, e.g., trucks and commercial vehicles, passenger cars and possibly other wheeled, nonfighting vehicles such as trailers and supply or medical units." The company would also encourage its *white* employees to "volunteer to join a local commando unit . . . The G.M. commando unit would assume guarding responsibility for the G.M. plants and would fall under the control of the local military authority for the duration of the emergency . . . " The G.M. contingency plan makes it clear that the corporation perceives its interests to be identical to those of the South African government. Although General Motors claims that the contingency plan is no longer in effect, it was, at *least* until 1978, official G.M. policy. Although General Motors signed the employment code written by a member of its own board, it seems highly unlikely that the Sullivan Principles will stand in the way of G.M.'s cozy relationship with the South African government.

Ford

Signatory companies are rated in terms of their implementation of the Sullivan Principles—not their degree of non-cooperation with the South African regime. Ford and General Motors fall short according to both criteria. Yet, Arthur D. Little considers them to be model signatory companies. In August 1979, after touring the South African subsidiaries of both Ford and General Motors, American civil rights activist, the Reverend Jesse Jackson, told the press that he was "not impressed" with their efforts to improve the conditions of black workers.* "They are doing too little in proportion to their potential," Jackson said. "There are still too few blacks in management and almost no blacks in major decision-making positions."[81]

Since Jackson's visit, the conditions at Ford have worsened. In November 1979, Ford Motor Company, one of the largest U.S. investors in South Africa and one of the biggest employers in the South African automotive industry, fired nearly all of the black workers in its Struandale Port Elizabeth plant. Seven hundred black workers were dismissed when they walked off their jobs in protest of racist treatment by white workers and the white officials who fill nearly all of the management and supervisory positions. Prior to the walk-out, Ford had posted notices indicating that refusal to do "reasonable overtime" would be regarded "as formal resignation." The company had also banned workers' meetings on factory property.

The forced resignation of Thozamile Botha, a black political activist, was the spark that ignited the Ford dispute. Botha, who was ultimately reinstated, listed some of the workers' grievances against the company:

For example, 'equal pay for equal work.' According to the company, we have it. In reality, what we have is equal grade for equal work—but with huge differences

---

*Reverend Jesse Jackson, a longtime civil rights activist who is currently the director of Operation PUSH, a Chicago-based community self-help organization, is not affiliated with the Sullivan monitoring group.

of pay within each grade, whites right at the top of the scale and blacks at the bottom.[82]

The workers also claimed that Ford consistently reserved the best jobs for whites, favored the whites in training programs, and refused to consider the black workers' grievances.

By January 1980, the situation surrounding the Ford dispute had deteriorated significantly. After months of tense negotiations, Ford finally agreed to reinstate the striking workers. A few days later, the South African security police raided a meeting of the Port Elizabeth Black Civic Organization, the activist group that had been organizing strikers at the Ford Motor plant. More than 20 PEBCO members were detained, including five members of the group's executive. PEBCO president and Ford activist, Thozamile Botha, was imprisoned. PEBCO vice president, Liso Pityana, was banned.[83] After spending nearly two months in prison, Botha and two other activists were released and banned under South Africa's *Internal Security Act.*[84]

According to Zakhele George Manase, national organizer of the black United Automobile, Rubber and Allied Workers' Union (UARAW), and national secretary of the Sullivan Principles monitoring committee, the attitudes and practices of other companies—such as General Motors—are no better than those at Ford. Manase stated that very little is being done to implement the Sullivan Principles in any of the signatory companies. There is no such thing as equal pay for equal work, he said. Discriminatory hiring practices are not being abolished. Manase further stated that his own union's progress is being hampered at General Motors by the personnel department, which is discouraging blacks from joining the union.[85]

Although the black UARAW *has* been recognized at Ford, the practices of the union have come under heavy criticism by Black Consciousness leaders and the striking workers at the Ford plant. At a press conference convened by Bishop Tutu in December 1979, then-president of the Azanian African People's Organization, C. Nkondo, called the black union at Ford "a glorified committee."

FORD VEHICLE SALES TO SOUTH AFRICAN PUBLIC SECTOR

Department/agency	1977	1976	1975	1974	1973
South African railways	87	679	1,357	736	490
Provincial administrations	401	543	980	654	551
Homelands	505	510	367	197	185
Police	308	369	425	649	566
Government transportation[1]	170	300	585	2,000	1,055
Namibia administration	113	224	103	92	131
Post office and other	358	284	463	125	101
TOTAL	1,942	2,909	4,280	4,453	3,079
Sales to Defense Ministry included above	120	100	90	205	207
Sales of U.S.-origin trucks to Defense Ministry	29	79	64	138	104
Sales of U.S.-origin trucks to police	240	246	243	418	435

1. Sales to Defense Ministry are included with Government transportation.

Note: In February 1978, in compliance with new Commerce Department export control regulations, all sales of U.S.-origin trucks to the South African police and military were halted.

Source: United States Private Investment in South Africa. U.S. Government Printing Office, 1978.

In spite of its prominent placement in Ford's public relations campaign, the UARAW has never signed a contract with the company and has no collective bargaining power.

Ford activist, Thozamile Botha, said that initially, the union had been reluctant to support the workers "because they said the strike was political." Dr. Nthato Motlana and C. Nkondo, who had pledged their support to the striking workers, linked the UARAW with the nationwide black trade union movement, which they condemned as a "spineless" movement without any real power.[86]

The weakness of the black trade union structure in South Africa is exemplified by the situation at Ford. In spite of its prominent placement in Ford's public relations campaign, the UARAW has never signed a contract with the company and has no collective bargaining power. The automotive company has never dealt with the union directly; it has merely allowed a black union representative to sit on the company's liaison committee, a negotiating committee composed of management and worker representatives that lacks the legal power to enforce its contracts. Because the Ford workers could not effectively air their grievances through "proper" channels, they walked off their jobs in protest. Ford officials justified their strike-busting actions with the rationale that the walk-out had not been sponsored by the black union "recognized" by Ford, and thus, could not be considered a legitimate strike.

Throughout the duration of the Ford dispute, the South African government rejected all forms of intervention by American critics. According to the *Johannesburg Star,* the government refused to allow Reverend Jesse Jackson to take a high-level delegation to South Africa to investigate the labor unrest. The delegation would have included such prominent Americans as Cardiss Collins, chairperson of the Congressional Black Caucus; Richard Hatcher, Mayor of Gary, Indiana; and Marc Stepp, vice president of the United Auto Workers, which is affiliated with the black UARAW in South Africa.[87] By denying the

American delegation access to the site of the labor unrest, the South African government was able to prevent an independent investigation of the company's activities. It was not even necessary to invoke the *Protection of Business Act* in order to squelch an inquiry into the discriminatory practices of a Sullivan signatory company.

The implications of the Ford strike have made a strong impact on the thoughts of some U.S. government officials. Upon returning from South Africa in January 1980, Senator Paul Tsongas told the press:

> *Ford had the most progressive hiring policies of all American companies and major companies in South Africa ... (Yet) Ford had the strike. Mr. Botha, who led the strike, has already been in jail 14 days with a number of his colleagues. If that happens to Ford, which everyone thinks of as the most liberal U.S. company, you can imagine what the potential is in some other plants ... The case of Ford Motor Company I think is devastating since they did adhere to reasonably good (employment) practices—and still it didn't work . . . The Sullivan Principles foundation in U.S. business, I don't think is worth anything.*[88]

An official of the U.S. executive branch stated emphatically that the Ford strike had sent "20 rounds of buckshot into the Sullivan Principles."[89]

The Computer Industry

Through the manipulation of legal loopholes, Ford and General Motors have managed to supply the strategic needs of the South African government without breaking U.S. law. Other companies have used less sophisticated methods. Control Data, for example, is considered to be "making good progress" in its implementation of the Sullivan Principles. On March 10, 1979, the *St. Louis Post-Dispatch* reported that the Minneapolis-based corporation had sold a major computer subsystem to a British firm, International Computers, Ltd., which incorporated it into a larger system that was sold to the South African

. . . the chairman of Control Data remarked, "The little bit of repression that is added by the computer in South Africa is hardly significant."

police. The police intend to use the ICL system to implement the pass laws—the cornerstone of the apartheid structure. Due to the subsystem's final destination, Control Data's Britain-to-South Africa sales violated the Commerce Department's 1978 export regulations. The *Post-Dispatch* cited internal Control Data papers documenting the company's awareness of this fact. The computer company, a top category Sullivan signatory, is helping to implement a system responsible for the arrest of nearly 300,000 black people in 1978 alone. Nonetheless, the chairman of Control Data remarked the following year, "The little bit of repression that is added by the computer in South Africa is hardly significant."[90]

Control Data is not the only American computer company making sales to the South African government. IBM, Hewlett-Packard, NCR, and Sperry Rand—all "making good progress"—and Burroughs and Honeywell, who are "making acceptable progress" in their implementation of the Sullivan Principles, include the South African government among their major clients. The Commerce Department regulations prohibiting sales to the South African security forces have eliminated only a fraction of their sales.

American computers are used in every major sector of the South African government and economy. According to C. Cotton, managing director of Burroughs South Africa,

> *We're entirely dependent on the U.S. The economy would grind to a halt without access to the computer technology of the West. No bank could function; the government couldn't collect its money and couldn't account for it; business couldn't operate; payrolls could not be paid. Retail and wholesale marketing and related services would be disrupted.*[91]

American firms control 70 percent of the computer market

in South Africa. IBM is the single largest supplier and servicer of data-processing equipment, controlling between 38 and 50 percent of the market. At least one-third of IBM's business is with the South African government.[92] IBM, Burroughs, and Sperry Rand have provided computers that implement the pass laws, control the flow of migratory labor, and link into the central data bank in Johannesburg that keeps tabs on all of South Africa's adult black population. All of South Africa's key industries—motor vehicles, petroleum, tire and rubber, mining, and banking and financing—are serviced by American computers. The National Petroleum Refiners, which oversees the highly strategic coal-to-oil (SASOL) conversion plants, and the Atomic Energy Board, which develops nuclear weapons as well as nuclear power systems, operate with the help of Sperry Rand computers. IBM and Control Data equipment are used by the government-owned Electricity Supply Commission (ESCOM) and the Iron and Steel Corporation (ISCOR), as well as the Council for Scientific and Industrial (military) Research. IBM computers service the Armaments Board and the central Johannesburg stock exchange.[93] Honeywell's major government customers include ISCOR and SASOL, accounting for 20 percent of the company's business in South Africa.[94]

Although American computer companies are no longer *officially* making sales to the South African security forces, their contributions to other aspects of the apartheid system are equally critical to its survival. Moreover, computer parts and systems sold to other government agencies or to private industry are frequently resold to the military and police establishments. To facilitate matters, the South African government has organized a cooperative network among computer sections in eight different government agencies. According to the head of the computer division at the Anglo-American Corporation,

> *There is no way the United States authorities will be able to prevent this capacity from being shared by the defense and police departments.*[95]

Although they provide the South African government   69

with important instruments for maintaining white supremacy, American computer companies are considered to be among the most promising signatories to the Sullivan Principles.

The Energy Industry

Caltex, Mobil, and Exxon

South Africa needs oil. Completely lacking in domestic reserves, South Africa is forced to import 90 percent of its petroleum requirements. Although the country relies heavily on coal, critical sectors of the economy cannot function without oil. If South Africa's oil supply were cut off and its 18-month reserves depleted, the transportation sector would be crippled; chemicals production would cease; farm equipment would be useless; and military and police operations would grind to a halt.

Three Sullivan signatory companies—Caltex, Mobil, and Exxon—control 45 percent of the oil market in South Africa. Caltex and Mobil alone control 42 percent of the country's oil refining capacity and 40 percent of the petroleum products market. These two companies, whose combined investments amounted to more than $650 million in 1978, own more than two-fifths of all U.S. assets in South Africa.[96]

In mid-1978, in the aftermath of the black township uprisings, Caltex completed a $135 million expansion project at its Cape Town refinery. The three-year project nearly doubled the capacity of the refinery and increased South Africa's total refining capacity by 11 percent. Meanwhile, Mobil had opened a new $2.3 million lubricant re-refining plant—the second largest in South Africa.[97] Both Mobil and Caltex are heavily involved in oil exploration, and Exxon is currently prospecting for uranium—endeavors which the South African government hopes will make the country less reliant on foreign oil and less vulnerable to international oil sanctions.

A ready supply of petroleum is considered to be a vital component of South Africa's national security apparatus. Consequently, the industry is closely regulated by the South African government. Mobil's South African attorneys advised the corporation that because

... oil is absolutely vital to enable the army to move, the navy to sail and the air force to fly, it is likely that a South African court would hold that it falls within ... the definition of munitions of war (emphasis added).[98]

Under the stipulations of the *National Supplies Procurement Act,* oil companies cannot impose any conditions on the sale of oil. According to Standard Oil of California, a joint-owner of Caltex,

It would be a crime under South Africa's laws were Caltex South Africa to undertake a commitment to not supply petroleum products for use by the South African military or any other branch of the South African government.[99]

For more than a decade, the South African subsidiaries of Mobil and Caltex sold oil to the illegal minority government in Rhodesia—in defiance of United Nations sanctions. Similarly, in the event of an international oil embargo against South Africa, Mobil, Caltex, and Exxon would be obligated to supply oil to South African military and police forces. In spite of their critical and willing support for the South African military-industrial complex, Mobil, Caltex, and Exxon are considered to be model Sullivan signatories, "making good progress" in their implementation of the fair employment code.

Fluor

The South African government began to prepare for international oil sanctions as early as 1955, when it first began experimenting with a new coal-to-oil conversion process. In 1973, following the announcement by OPEC countries that they would no longer sell oil to South Africa, the minority government began to expand its coal-to-oil conversion capability. In 1975, it began construction of a second coal-to-oil conversion plant (SASOL II) under the direction of the government-owned South African Coal, Oil and Gas Corporation.

The California-based Fluor Corporation, one of the world's largest engineering and construction firms, was awarded major contracts on both the SASOL II plant and

71

the SASOL II Extension, initiated in 1979.* The SASOL II Extension, which will concentrate on the production of transport fuels, is expected to provide 30 to 50 percent of South Africa's oil requirements by 1983.† Together, the Fluor contracts are worth approximately $4.2 billion.

The Fluor Corporation's role in the SASOL II Extension is critical. Its contractual obligations include "the management and coordination of the total project, including a major portion of the engineering design, procurement, construction and a multitude of other supportive functions."[101] It will provide South Africa with technological expertise and equipment that may cut years off its program for strategic self-sufficiency. However, as a new signatory to the Sullivan Principles, the Fluor Corporation will do little to benefit South Africa's black population. According to a recent report in *Southern Africa*, an estimated 4,500 black workers will be hired during the first stage of the SASOL II Extension construction. Nearly three-quarters of these workers will mine coal, one of the lowest paying, most dangerous jobs in South Africa.[102] Compared to these minimal job opportunities, Fluor's contribution to the apartheid economy is quite substantial. As for the company's commitment to the Sullivan Principles, political and economic change are not even an issue for the Board of Directors. In a 1979 statement to Fluor stockholders, the Board stated:

> *Historically, the company has always abided by the laws, regulations and social customs of the country in which it works, and the management intends for the company to continue in this manner.*[103]

---

*In 1973, all of the OPEC countries, with the exception of Iran, prohibited the sale of oil to South Africa. Iran was South Africa's major oil supplier until early 1979, when the new Iranian government joined the OPEC oil embargo. Shortly thereafter, the South African government announced its plans for a multi-billion dollar SASOL II Extension project.

† Control Data and Honeywell are two of several other American companies involved in the SASOL II Extension project. Control Data will supply Fluor with a mainframe computer unit for its operations at the SASOL plant. Honeywell has a $13.8 million multi-year contract with SASOL to provide the plant with process control instrumentation.[100]

The Military Apparatus

Although oil is critical to many sectors of the South African economy, the transport sector is almost totally dependent on oil for its energy needs. It is estimated that oil provides 79 percent of the energy requirements in the transport sector, much of which is consumed by the South African security forces.[104] Mobil, Caltex, Exxon, and Fluor are not only bolstering South Africa's energy capabilities; they are the primary producers of *oil*, the lifeblood of the South African military apparatus.

Olin

Signatories to the Sullivan Principles have supplied fuel to the South African security forces, and they have equipped them with advanced military technology and weaponry. The Olin Corporation, for example, has signed the Sullivan Principles, and its South African subsidiaries are considered to be "making acceptable progress" in their implementation. However, between 1972 and 1975, Olin violated United States law and a United Nations embargo by shipping 3,200 firearms and 20 million rounds of ammunition to South Africa. In March 1978, Olin pleaded no contest to 21 criminal charges stemming from its illegal arms transfers. Two stockholder suits have subsequently been filed against the corporation, one seeking $4.8 million in damages on the grounds that the value of Olin's stock was falsely inflated when its increased earnings were attributed to good management, when in fact, they were due to the illegal arms sales to South Africa.[105]

In spite of its flagrant violations of U.S. law, the Olin Corporation was given kid-glove treatment by the federal government. The arms manufacturer was fined only $510,000, to be paid to local charities as "reparations" for its misdeeds. The leniency of the penalty is particularly evident when compared with the corporation's annual earnings from arms manufactures. While the $510,000 fine was intended to compensate for illegal activities that spanned a period of four years, Olin earned $300 million from arms sales worldwide in 1977 alone.[106]

As in the case of the Space Research Corporation, 73

Olin was given immunity from certain federal regulations. On the day of the company's conviction, the U.S. Treasury Department granted it "relief" from a federal law that would have revoked its license to manufacture and sell arms. According to an attorney in the Treasury Department's Alcohol, Tobacco and Firearms division, relief cannot be granted if continuation of the license is either "dangerous to public safety" or "contrary to the public interest." However, the attorney continued, "As far as public safety (is concerned) a corporation is just a piece of paper; it can't go out and shoot anybody."[107] Furthermore, the company claimed, the shut-down of Olin's arms manufacturing division, which accounts for 20 percent of the corporation's total sales, would cause serious hardships for Olin's workers and stockholders.*[108]

It is Olin U.S.A., not its South African subsidiaries, that sold arms to the apartheid government. It was the Olin parent company that signed the Sullivan Principles, and the parent company that is responsible for monitoring them. While the U.S. firm is gun-running to South Africa, its subsidiaries contribute very little to the welfare of the black worker. According to a report prepared by the American Consulate General in Johannesburg, one of Olin's subsidiaries, a chemical manufacturing plant, employs only 14 workers. The other subsidiary is not even mentioned.[110] Nonetheless, the Arthur D. Little Company still considers Olin to be "making acceptable progress" in its implementation of the Sullivan Principles, a code intended to bring about racial equality and justice.

*Olin's concern for its employees was noticeably absent in its treatment of striking workers at its New Haven, Connecticut plant in the summer of 1979. In July 1979, 1,350 Olin workers walked off their jobs in protest of a new speed-up clause that would have put a large number of older and handicapped employees out of work. When the workers, represented by the International Association of Machinists, refused to comply with a back-to-work ultimatum, Olin began to hire non-union employees to replace them. Policemen in riot gear broke through the union blockade so that non-union workers could enter the factory. The Machinists accused the company of using "gestapo" strike-breaking tactics—limiting the number of pickets, tacking barbed wire on the gates, videotaping the strikers, and requiring them to register their names and wear armbands.[109]

74

Motorola was not selling the South African police its best equipment, the officials said—only its second best. The most sophisticated items they reserved for the Chicago police.

Motorola

Olin, Space Research, and Control Data are but a few of the American companies that have supplied the apartheid government with strategic technology. At the same time that the Control Data scandal was unfolding in 1978, Chicago activists were meeting with the Illinois-based Motorola Corporation to discuss that company's involvement in South Africa. The Motorola executives hotly defended their South African activities, which include the manufacture and sale of automotive parts, two-way radios, and data and control systems. Motorola was not selling the South African police its *best* equipment, the officials said—only its *second* best. The most sophisticated items they reserved for the *Chicago* police—a department with one of the highest police/civilian kill ratios in the country.[111] Motorola is another Sullivan signatory that is considered to be "making acceptable progress" in its implementation of a code that is supposed "to bring about the downfall of apartheid without violence."[112]

Armed Aggression Against Its Neighbors

American arms, weapons technology, and electronic equipment have been critical factors in South Africa's repression of its own people. American technical and economic assistance have enabled the apartheid government to defend its system beyond South African borders, launching continuous armed attacks into Namibia, Angola, Zambia, and Mozambique. While the minority regime attempts to mold its border states into a constellation of moderate, economically dependent nations, American corporations contribute the goods and technology that supply the South African security forces.

Since P.W. Botha became prime minister in September 1978, there has been a dramatic increase in South African attacks on neighboring countries. According to a United Nations Security Council report, the South African defense forces were responsible for 94 air space violations, 21 ground infiltrations, 21 border provocations, 7 artillery bombardments, 193 armed mine-laying operations, 25 attacks by ground forces, 24 aerial bombardments, and one large combined operation involving ground and air forces in Angola between March 1976 and June 1979.[113] For three years, the South African government has given continuous economic backing and intermittant troop support to the UNITA forces in their efforts to destabilize Angola's Marxist government.

In violation of United Nations sanctions, the South African government spent $50 million a month in Rhodesia to help the rebel regime combat the Patriotic Front liberation forces.[114] There have been numerous reports of South African pilots, technicians, and "volunteers" in Rhodesia, as well as extensive cooperation between their military and intelligence commands. In September and October 1979, South African and Rhodesian forces staged a series of "anti-guerrilla" raids into Mozambique, Zambia, and Angola, taking hundreds of civilian lives, destroying bridges, agricultural areas, and powerlines.[115] Meanwhile, Zambia was economically isolated, its external rail links destroyed, and its vital shipments of maize cut off. Intolerant of its neighbors' support for the Zimbabwean and Namibian liberation movements, the apartheid government is using its vast military and economic might to force them into political and economic subservience.

Bank Loans to South Africa

Each trade agreement, each bank loan, each new investment is another brick in the wall of our continued existence.

J.B. Vorster, former
Prime Minister of South Africa

Citicorp

76   South Africa's acts of foreign aggression and internal

repression would not be possible without the help of international bank loans. In order to accommodate its expanding military operations and cope with mounting civil unrest, the South African government augmented its defense budget from $688 million in 1973 to more than $2 billion in 1979—an increase of nearly 300 percent. At the end of 1976, South Africa was in debt to American banks to the tune of $2.2 billion—approximately equal to the amount of foreign exchange required to cover its soaring defense expenditures and oil import bill.[116]

Throughout the 1970's, Citicorp, the largest banking organization in America, was South Africa's top international lender. Between 1972 and 1978, the corporation participated in banking consortia that made $1.6 billion in loans to the South African government and its agencies.[117] In 1979, Citicorp reported $401 million in outstanding loans to the South African government, its agencies, and private industries in South Africa—amounting to one-quarter of the total U.S. loans outstanding to South Africa.[118]

Citicorp loans to South African agencies have been strategically placed. The corporation has made loans worth hundreds of millions of dollars to the government-owned Iron and Steel Corporation (ISCOR), which meets 72 percent of the country's iron and steel requirements; the Electricity Supply Commission (ESCOM), which is undertaking the construction of two new nuclear reactors; the government-controlled South African Broadcasting Corporation; and the Industrial Development Corporation, which is responsible for the development and expansion of South Africa's strategic industries. In the private sector, Citicorp has made extensive loans to the mining industry, the most vital sector of the South African economy.[119]

The size and strategic placement of Citicorp loans are paralleled by the critical timing of the transactions. Major loans were made to the South African public and private sectors following the Sharpeville Massacre of 1960 and the Soweto uprisings of 1976. At a time when political instability threatened to deter foreign investors, Citicorp came to the rescue and helped pull the country through a severe economic crisis. Assured by Citicorp's generous

77

loans that South Africa remained a good investment opportunity, multinational corporations once again poured capital into the apartheid economy.

Since March 1978, Citicorp has made loans only to the private sector in South Africa, stating that apartheid has "a negative effect on South Africa's economic viability."[120] However, the corporation has refused to suspend all lending to South Africa on the grounds that such action is a political, rather than an economic, decision.[121] Thus, Citicorp continues to make trade-related loans, many of which are military or strategic in function (e.g., loans to buy "non-military" Cessna and Atlas aircraft—whose function is to patrol South African borders and engage in "reconnaissance" missions over Angola).[122] It continues to make loans to private industry, and, it has reserved the right to reinstitute loans to the South African public sector in the event that the economy reaches a new equilibrium. If the soaring price of gold brings renewed strength and growth to the apartheid economy, Citicorp may well decide that loans to the minority government are worth any incumbent risk.

Not only is Citicorp the largest U.S. lender to South Africa, it is the only American bank with subsidiaries in that country. Through its wholly-owned subsidiary, Citibank, N.A., Citicorp has operated in South Africa since 1958. With branches in Johannesburg, Cape Town, and Durban, the corporation has investments in South Africa worth more than $13.1 million. Citibank, N.A. is the twelfth largest bank in South Africa.[123]

According to South African law, all banks in South Africa must invest 15 percent of their public assets in South African government bonds.[124] Its lending policies aside, the very presence of Citibank in South Africa contributes to the strength of the white minority regime. In a general statement on foreign operations, Citicorp has made it clear that it does not look adversely on such close cooperation with host country governments:

We must never lose sight of the fact that we are guests in foreign countries. We must conduct ourselves accordingly. Local governments can pass any kind of legislation, and whether we like it or not, we must conform to it.

Under these circumstances, <u>Citibank can survive</u> *<u>only if we are successful in demonstrating to the local</u>* *<u>authorities that our presence is useful to them</u> (em-* *phasis added).*[125]

That Citibank, N.A. has been useful to the South African government is beyond question. Whether or not its involvement in the South African economy has been beneficial to the black population is another issue altogether.

Citibank, N.A. was one of the first signatories to the Sullivan Principles, and, according to the third compliance report, it is "making good progress" in their implementation. Although the bank is considered to be a top-category Sullivan signatory, its workforce is disproportionately white. In June 1979, 73 percent of Citibank's employees were white; 16 percent were black. None of the blacks were employed in managerial or supervisory positions, and only one bank officer—out of a total of 36—was black. Citibank's training programs focused on its 78 professional, supervisory, and management employees— 71 of whom were white. Between January and June 1979, only two blacks participated in Citibank's job training programs.[126] That Citibank has made "progress" in implementing the Sullivan employment reforms is, at best, questionable. Compared to the vital function of its parent company in sustaining the apartheid economy, Citibank's record of workplace reforms is, at most, insignificant.

A Progressive Force for White South Africa

The infusion of foreign capital into the South African economy has stimulated considerable growth in the country's gross national product, increased its repressive capacities, and beefed up its war machine. Yet, these investments have had little positive impact on mounting black unemployment. Between 1970 and 1976, black unemployment in the urban areas and white rural areas grew from 6.1 percent to 10.9 percent. In the white rural areas alone, 1.7 percent of the blacks were unemployed in

1970, while 22.1 percent were unemployed in 1976.[127] In 1978, nearly one-third of the black South African workforce was unemployed.[128] Even these figures are overly optimistic since there is no official record of unemployed blacks in the African homelands, where the vast majority of the people have no jobs and barely eke a living from the worn-out land. Although South Africa's GNP increased in the 1970's, black workers have received an ever-diminishing share.

The paradox of increased economic growth, coupled with a decreased need for labor, is peculiar to highly-advanced technological societies. The South African economy is characterized by capital-intensive industries that seldom contribute to, and often eliminate, job opportunities for the black majority. A prime example of such an industry is Richard's Bay Minerals, a $290 million mining and smelting operation in the KwaZulu homeland. The enterprise is partially controlled by the Quebec Iron and Titanium Company of Canada, which has a 40 percent interest in the operation. The remaining 60 percent is divided between the South African government-owned Industrial Development Corporation and the Union Corporation, a major South African mining house. Quebec Iron and Titanium is owned by two American corporations, the Kennecott Copper Company (66.5 percent) and Gulf and Western Industries (33.5 percent).

Kennecott Copper is a signatory to the Sullivan Principles, and, according to the October 1979 report, it is "making acceptable progress" in their implementation. However, Kennecott's subsidiary operations in Richard's Bay are having very little impact on the socio-economic development of the KwaZulu homeland. The homeland has a population of 2.1 million people, only 27 percent of whom are economically active in the homeland. Their earnings account for a mere 25 percent of the KwaZulu people's total income.[129] Because the South African government has severely restricted the number, type, and location of African businesses, most of these earnings are ultimately returned to the white economy.

Although Richard's Bay Minerals will eventually provide approximately 650 jobs for blacks, the South African government estimates that 30,400 local jobs must be created *each year* in order to absorb the population of migratory laborers from KwaZulu. Kennecott Copper's capital-intensive investment will not begin to reverse the outflow of labor from the homeland. Moreover, very little of the operation's profits will return to the homeland government; the KwaZulu Investment Corporation will receive 10 percent of the profits as payment for exploitation of the land.[130]

It cannot be expected that a single corporation solve all of the problems of apartheid. However, the benefits of the corporation to black South Africa must be carefully weighed against its contribution to the apartheid system. Richard's Bay Minerals will ultimately employ 650 black workers. At the same time, its export potential is estimated to be worth $115 million *per year*. The generation of foreign exchange is critical to the government's ability to repay more than $9 billion in international bank loans. The development and expansion of its mining industry is a decisive factor in South Africa's program of strategic self-sufficiency. The creation of a few hundred jobs, most of which will involve unskilled mining labor, cannot counterbalance the corporation's vital support of the apartheid structure. Given the strategic nature of Kennecott's investment in the South African economy, it is difficult to consider the corporation a "progressive force" for change.

CHAPTER III
IMPROVING UPON APARTHEID: THE SEMBLANCE OF REFORM

Blacks see foreign investors as deliberately blind to inequities of the South African social system and indeed prepared to profit by it through low wages and submissive force it offers ... Even if foreign firms offer minor reforms, it is only to create comfortable black middle class which will perpetuate exploitation of African masses ...

> Confidential Cable from U.S.
> Ambassador William Bowdler, to the
> State Department, March 1977

Reform is illusory in South Africa. Modifications in the work environment and superficial changes in trade union laws do not alter the basic structure of apartheid. The homelands policy remains intact. Migratory labor, influx control, and the pass laws continue unabated. South Africa's black millions remain disenfranchised and dispossessed, while American companies continue to reap the benefits of a "good investment climate." Workplace reforms do not alter the strategic importance of American companies to the South African economy. They do not weaken the links of corporate collaboration or soften the blows of government repression. These adjustments in apartheid simply serve to fragment the black community.

Modifications in the workplace environment are enabling a small black elite to enter South Africa's economic mainstream. Although their labor continues to be exploited, and profits are still made at their expense, these elites are tossed the crumbs of economic growth. While they are still denied citizenship and fundamental

In order to ensure the continuation of white minority dominance in South Africa, the government has implemented a series of laws designed to prevent the black, Asian, and colored people from uniting against the white minority.

economic, political, and social rights, they have a stake in the altered system.

The division of the black population and the creation of elites within it is not a phenonomenon unique to workplace reforms; the South African government has been implementing "divide and rule" policies since the formation of the Union in 1910. In order to ensure the continuation of white minority dominance in South Africa, the government has implemented a series of laws designed to prevent the black, Asian, and colored people from uniting against the white minority. Since the early part of the century, the black population has been divided into homelands and urban barracks according to tribe. In subsequent years, Asians and coloreds were separated from native blacks and confined to ghettoes in the "white" areas of the country.

Since the Asian and colored populations are not forced to live in homelands or townships, are not subject to influx control and pass laws, and are not controlled by the migratory labor system, they have been considered more privileged population groups than the native Africans. However, they are by no means first class South African citizens. Asians and coloreds are not represented in the national parliament. They cannot hold public office. They are barred from high-level skilled work and wages that are comparable to those of whites. They are denied entrance into "white" schools, residential areas, and "public" facilities. Like South Africa's 18.6 million blacks, Asians and coloreds are simply cogs in the wheel of the white economy.

According to Wilson Shuyenyane, director of a South African leadership exchange program, the new government-business reform program is simply another

> *. . . one of those tactics to create constant divisions in the black people . . . We are split nationally and culturally and now they want to do it economically.*[131]

Another middle class black, who works as a public relations officer in a large South African food company, said the sentiments expressed by Shuyenyane prevail in the black townships:

> *The militant students hate the term "middle class" because they say it makes people forget. They see the middle class as a tool of the status quo, and they do have a point there.*[132]

The Sullivan reforms and similar government-initiated measures serve to strengthen, rather than minimize, the divisions within the non-white population. They are helping to create a class of non-whites with a vested interest in the reformed system, a stake in society that will make its members "natural" allies of the white-controlled political and economic structures. In the event of black rebellion or revolution, this class could help to protect the interests of the white minority against the non-white majority of the population. In the face of black unrest and rising demands for economic and social change, white South Africa hopes, and American businesses believe, that workplace reforms will be enough. If the government-business coalition can divide the black population through token change and stave off revolution by patching up the old system, their gamble will have been a success.

For the United States government, the issue is not that simple. American policy has always favored any government that is a moderate stabilizing force, a regime that is anti-Soviet, willing to protect American investments, supply the U.S. with important minerals, and play Western policeman in the Southern Hemisphere. Unfortunately, such prerequisites for American friendship have placed the United States on the wrong side of the liberation struggle. The United States has become integrally tied to a racist government that is fighting the forces of black liberation and nationalism, thwarting the advent of black majority rule. As United States investments increase in South Africa and the stability of the region continues to deteriorate, American commitment to the minority regime will expand accordingly. At the same time, the pressures of world opinion will require that the government "act tough" on South Africa, threatening punitive action in response to its repressive racial policies. As a result, the United States government, like American business, has embraced the employment code, hoping that the semblance of criticism will obviate the need for more rigorous action.

The idea of patching up apartheid through employment reform is not derived from the South African experience. Similar techniques were used to smooth over the inequities of the American economic system throughout the 1960's and '70's. In 1964, the United States Congress passed the *Civil Rights Act* and created the Equal Employment Opportunity Commission (EEOC) to monitor business compliance with the equal employment opportunity clause (Title VII). While the EEOC was granted the power to file suit against American companies with discriminatory employment practices, the fundamental inequities of the American economic system were left undisturbed. The commission could not alter the fact that Americans presented with "equal employment opportunities" rarely compete against the same odds, or that determinants such as race, class, and sex begin working at birth, not at age 16.

Business, meanwhile, took advantage of the reformist mood. At the height of the civil rights era, "affirmative action" hiring practices could only enhance its public image. Women and blacks were brought in to decorate the board rooms and executive suites, while control of the enterprises remained in the hands of the entrenched power structure. In actuality, the changes simply meant business as usual—the old system with a new face. The old structures of unequal accumulation, distribution, and decision-making power remained intact. The labor of many continued to make profits for the few.

American companies are quick to compare the situations in the United States and in South Africa. If the civil rights problem was licked in America, they say, the

85

same techniques should be applied in South Africa. Take down the "Jim Crow" signs. Integrate the cafeterias and toilets. Train a few more blacks for skilled positions, and condemn the practice of racial discrimination. Once again, the corporate argument falls short. In the United States, the problem of discrimination focuses on a minority of the population; in South Africa, three-quarters of the population is denied equality of opportunity—solely on the basis of race. Yet, the solutions of the 1960's have not even worked in America. The inequities of American life—poverty, hunger, unemployment, and illiteracy—are still distributed largely according to race, even though the principles of equal employment opportunity are written into U.S. law. In South Africa, corporate endorsement of and compliance with the employment code is purely voluntary, and is certainly not encouraged by the South African legal system.

Corporate signatories to the Sullivan Principles insist that, although the code is voluntary, they will take it seriously. The domestic records of these firms cast doubt on their sincerity. Between 1973 and 1979, the following Sullivan signatory companies entered into court approved consent decrees with the Equal Employment Opportunity Commission for the violation of U.S. equal employment opportunity law:

Abbott Laboratories
American Cyanamid Co.
Armco Steel Corp.
Bethlehem Steel Corp.
Borden Inc.
Celanese Corp.
Crown Cork & Seal Co.
Dow Chemical Co.
FMC Corp.
Ford Motor Co.
General Electric
General Motors Corp.
Grolier Inc.
Heublein Inc.
Honeywell Inc.

IBM Corp.

International Harvester Co.
International Telephone & Telegraph
Johnson Control International Inc.
Kellogg Co.
Minnesota Mining & Manufacturing Co.
Mobil Oil Corp.
Monsanto Co.
NCR Corp.
Otis Elevator Co.
Phillips Petroleum Co.
Rockwell International Corp.
Singer Co.
Sperry Corp.
Uniroyal Inc.
Upjohn Co.
Westinghouse Electric Corp.
W.R. Grace Co.[133]

The above list does not include those signatory companies whose suits were settled out of court.

Since the passage of the U.S. *Civil Rights Act* in 1964, the American business community has tried to prevent the EEOC from becoming an effective enforcement agency. In a letter to Senator Richard Russell, written in 1964, Walter Carey, president of the U.S. Chamber of Commerce, stated that:

> *The national chamber recommends that the powers of the Equal Employment Opportunity Commission be limited to conciliation and persuasion. We are very dubious about the value of court proceedings and orders to accomplish the hoped-for results.*[134]

In the late 1960's, members of the U.S. Chamber of Commerce and several national business associations lobbied against a bill designed to grant greater enforcement powers to the EEOC. During the summer of 1978, a dozen representatives of major Sullivan signatory companies testified before two House subcommittees in opposition to a bill that would have incorporated the terms of the U.S. *Civil Rights Act* into legislation regulating the practices of American subsidiaries in

87

. . . the same American companies that have dragged their heels on domestic reform promise that they will voluntarily negotiate with black trade unions in South Africa and pay black workers equal wages for equal work.

South Africa. The bill was never brought to a vote.

American companies have made it clear that they prefer to monitor their own employment practices, using their own yardsticks for progress. They would prefer equal employment policies to be voluntary—devoid of penalties for non-compliance. They insist that such policies would be adequate in South Africa, although in the United States, where fair employment practices are enforceable by law, the results have been far from earth-shaking. Sixteen years after the passage of the U.S. *Civil Rights Act,* ethnic minorities still compose the bulk of the unskilled labor force. Increases in income, job training, and advancement have been painfully slow in coming. Yet, the same American companies that have dragged their heels on domestic reform promise that they will voluntarily negotiate with black trade unions in South Africa and pay black workers equal wages for equal work. They claim that they will promote fair hiring practices, even though they were attracted to South Africa by the profits to be gained through the exploitation of black labor.

Signatory practices belie their words. There are no equal employment practices in their South African subsidiaries. Equal pay for equal work, black trade union rights, non-discriminatory hiring and promotion practices—all are virtually non-existent. As long as the issue of citizenship is side-stepped and the question of economic justice ignored, these corporations will continue to sustain the system of white minority rule. Their employment "reforms" will remain a sham—and the Sullivan Principles, a flimsy camouflage to disguise corporate collaboration with the apartheid regime.

AFTERWORD

A NEW STRATEGY FOR APARTHEID

In South Africa, the interests of government and business go hand-in-hand. Both need blacks who are skilled—but not *too* skilled—who are educated, but only enough to do their jobs. They need a black labor force that feels it has a stake in the system—too much to lose if something went wrong, but not enough to forget that they have it by privilege and not by right. They need a new class of blacks who will serve as a buffer between white interests and the impoverished millions in the townships and homelands—a small group of elites who will not protest present conditions for fear of being pushed back into the reservoir of the unemployed.

Prominent members of the South African government have been outspoken in their support of policies that would create a black buffer class. Addressing a group of Afrikaner businessmen in 1979, Minister of Cooperation and Development, Pieter Koornhof, said,*

> *The important point is that the level of progress that could develop among blacks in a free enterprise system should be so advantageous that chaos and revolution would hold such risks that blacks would fight against it.*[135]

Simond Brand, Prime Minister Botha's top economic advisor, voiced a similar opinion:

*The Department of Cooperation and Development was formerly entitled, the "Department of Plural Relations," and prior to that, the "Department of Bantu Affairs."

Blacks must be allowed to take part fully in the free enterprise system if we want them to accept it and defend it and make it their own . . . It is an implied intention to create a black middle class . . .[136]

The introduction of conduct codes for South African companies is part of a conscious government-business strategy to create a black buffer and to protect the apartheid economy. The Sullivan Principles were neither the first nor the last of these business codes. In 1974, the British government instituted a code of conduct for United Kingdom subsidiaries in South Africa. The U.K. code served as a model for the European Economic Community (EEC) code, adopted by the nine member nations in 1977. The Canadian government developed a similar code in 1978. In South Africa, the business community, under the auspices of the Urban Foundation and the South African Consultative Committee on Labor Affairs (SACCOLA), recommended a more general employment code, specifically stating that all reforms must occur within the "South African legal framework."

In conjunction with the business codes, the South African government introduced its own program of reform. Following the black township uprisings of 1976, the government announced the formation of two commissions to study the conditions that precipitated the urban unrest. The work of the commissions was solidly supported by the South African business community, whose interests were seriously threatened by the growing militancy of urban blacks, and by advocates of the Sullivan Principles, who were hard-pressed to provide answers to their opponents' criticisms. The task of the commissions was to "get beyond Sullivan," to provide a South African solution to South African problems.

The Wiehahn Commission

The commission headed by Professor Nicholas Wiehahn was charged with the study of a broad range of labor laws affecting black workers, and ultimately, with making recommendations for "the adjustment of the existing system." In spite of the complementary nature of government and business efforts, Professor Wiehahn was irritated by the implementation of *foreign* employment codes, considering them to be unwarranted intervention into South African affairs. In an interview with *South African Outlook,* Wiehahn enumerated some of his criticism of the codes:

> . . . *These codes, firstly, constitute gross forms of interference in an almost 'sacrosanct' relationship, i.e. between employer and employee. In a free market economy, this relationship should be left almost entirely to those two parties—the State should not interfere—least of all foreign states . . . Finally, the fact that they virtually compel employers to encourage Black trade unionism—the traditional rivals of employers—is contrary to a basic premise of labour science, namely that each party in the labour conflict situation should draw its growth and development from its own inner strength.*[137]

Professor Wiehahn's statement is a classic example of the convoluted thinking that characterizes South African racial reforms. The disruption of the "free market economy" constitutes the very essence of apartheid. The South African government has consistently interfered in the labor sphere—reserving thousands of skilled jobs for white workers, denying black workers access to training and apprenticeship programs, refusing to recognize black trade unions, restricting the right of black workers to strike, requiring the segregation of workplace facilities, and maintaining tight control over the flow of black labor into the urban environment. Under the *Industrial Conciliation Act of 1924,* the government has even denied black workers recognition as "employees." Given the high level of government involvement in the labor relations process, its severe restrictions on black entrepreneurial and property ownership rights, and its control of strategic economic sectors through investments in giant public corporations, it is outright deception to claim that South Africa is a "free market economy."

Although Wiehahn personally called upon black workers to rely on their "own inner strength" in the face of these restrictions, the Wiehahn Commission ultimately recommended that the government recognize black trade unions. This proposal, one of the few that has actually been approved by the South African government, has been widely acclaimed as a step forward in the elimination of petty apartheid. Its purpose, however, is not greater protection for black workers, but stricter government control. The Wiehahn recommendations are designed to eliminate all political activity within the black trade union structures.

In the course of the past decade, militant black trade unions have attained a membership of nearly 70,000 workers. Many of these unions have strong links to the Black Consciousness Movement and substantial political and financial backing abroad. As long as these unions are not recognized by law, they are immune from the statutory prohibition against labor organizations engaging in political activities. Since the *Unlawful Organizations Act of 1960* forbids the establishment of black political organizations per se, the decimation of the independent trade union movement would seriously weaken the base of black political activity inside South Africa. The destruction of this power base is the purpose of the Wiehahn Commission's plan.[138]

Under the new trade union laws, registered black unions will organize, develop, and perhaps disband under the watchful eye of the South African government. The Industrial Registrar has been given broad and arbitrary powers in approving and denying trade union registration. If the union does not "serve to maintain peace and harmony within the undertaking, industry, trade or occupation, and the national interest in general," it can be denied registration. Registration can be revoked at any time, enabling the government to silence militant organizations.[139] Union leaders are still liable to banning orders and "endorsement" back to the homelands.

According to the recommendations of the Wiehahn Commission, white trade unions will continue to dominate the workplace. They can deny workers union membership solely on the basis of race. "Closed shop" agreements between the dominant white unions and their employers will not be disturbed, effectively excluding black workers from apprenticeship programs and tens of thousands of skilled positions.

Any union that chooses to admit migrant workers will have the power to restrict the voting rights of these members; migrant workers make up one-third of the black workforce in urban areas. Moreover, trade unions that are represented on the Industrial Council can deny representation to newly-registered trade unions. As a final safeguard for continued white trade union domination, the South African government has encouraged the formation of black unions under the auspices of existing white unions. Accorded little actual power, the real purpose of the "parallel" union structure is to appease the black labor force and assuage international criticism, without diminishing white union control of the workplace.

The Riekert Commission

The Riekert Commission, charged with the study of manpower utilization, was the second of the government commissions established in the aftermath of the township uprisings. In May 1979, the Riekert Commission recommended the continuation of the influx control and the pass law systems—with some minor adjustments. The Commission report stated that "controlled employment and controlled accommodation are the two pillars on which the ordering of the urbanization process and sound and orderly community development ought to rest."[140] It recommended that employers be heavily fined for hiring blacks living in white areas without the proper passes, replacing the current system that penalizes illegal workers directly.

Acting upon the advice of the Riekert Commission, the South African government instituted a new maximum fine of $575 as a penalty for hiring an illegal worker. The result, according to Bishop Desmond Tutu, General Secretary of the South African Council of Churches, is that thousands of blacks are being fired from their jobs and "dumped like sacks of potatoes" into the homelands—where there are no jobs, no food, and only a scant supply of housing.[141] Sheena Duncan, director of the   93

Johannesburg Advice Office of the Black Sash, an organization that provides employment, housing, and legal advice to black urban dwellers, said the new law may be "the final straw which precipitate(s) disaster ... Never in the sixteen years since this office was opened have we experienced such anger expressed by Black people or such a sense of impending castastrophe."[142]

At the same time that it recommended increased control over blacks without urban residency rights, the Riekert Commission suggested that the government ease its restrictions on those who have the legal right to live there. As a result, the government has announced that if a black man with residency rights buys a house—a "privilege" granted in 1978—his wife can come and live with him. However, so few blacks can afford a home that a total of 30 have been purchased throughout South Africa in the year that the black home-ownership scheme has been in effect. A man cannot join the nine-year-long waiting list for rental accommodations unless his wife has a permit to live in the area—and she cannot get a permit until he has a house. Even if blacks had the financial means to take advantage of their new "rights," only a fraction of the black population would be affected. Out of nearly 19 million black people in South Africa, only 1.5 million have permanent urban residency rights.[143]

Plugging the Loopholes

The Wiehahn and Riekert Commissions, unlike Leon Sullivan, were charged with changing South Africa's "laws and customs." They plugged the most obvious loopholes in the employment codes and proposed an alteration in apartheid's facade. They recommended a modification of influx control and trade union laws for eight percent of the population—and were touted as a progressive force inside South Africa. However, both Wiehahn and Riekert further proposed that the 17.5 million blacks who do not have permanent urban residency rights not be accorded such "privileged" treatment. Illegal residents of urban areas should be deprived of their jobs and homes. Unregistered trade unions—those that failed or refused to comply with government regulations—should be stripped

94

. . . the charade of change has deceived no one. . . . Black leaders have likened the government and corporate reforms to "gilding the prison" and "rearranging the deck chairs on the Titanic."

of their power bases. The purpose of the government commissions, like that of the corporate reformers, is to lay the foundation for a new class of blacks—a slightly more privileged group who would "have something to lose if anything went wrong in South Africa."[144]

For Wiehahn, Riekert, and Sullivan, the dismantling of apartheid has never been an issue. Rather, they are seeking to "modernize" apartheid and to construct safety valves to relieve urban pressure. Their goal is to counter the growing disenchantment of the black population and to create new structures that will assure potential investors that the underlying causes for political instability are being resolved. In the post-reform era, investment in South Africa will once again be profitable and secure.

Since the Wiehahn and Riekert Commission reports were released in May 1979, more than $720 million of new capital has flowed into South Africa. However, the charade of change has deceived no one. Prime Minister Botha has assured white South Africa that "One man, one vote is out in this country. That is, never."[145] Black leaders have likened the government and corporate reforms to "gilding the prison" and "rearranging the deck chairs on the Titanic." Nthato Motlana, chairman of the Soweto Committee of Ten, has warned that, "The depth and range of anger is more widespread than before June 16"— the date of the 1976 Soweto uprising.[146] Black South Africa knows that the programs of Wiehahn, Riekert, and Sullivan are fueling the apartheid regime. It knows that the reforms are part of the government-corporate plan to divide the black population and ensure white minority rule. It knows, too, that the reformist days are numbered. Black South Africans will not continue to suffer for adjustments in apartheid, nor forego their basic rights for improvements upon a racist system.

APPENDIX I
SIGNATORIES TO THE
SULLIVAN PRINCIPLES
(October 1979)

Category I. Making Good Progress*
Caltex Petroleum Corporation
    Caltex Oil (S.A.) (Pty) Ltd.
The Chase Manhattan Bank
    Chase Manhattan Overseas Corporation
Citibank
    Citibank N.A. Ltd.
Colgate-Palmolive Company
    Colgate-Palmolive Ltd.
    Helena Rubinstein (S.A.)
Control Data Corporation
    Control Data Ltd. S.A.
Deere & Company
    John Deere (Pty) Ltd.
Eastman-Kodak Company
    Kodak (S.A.) (Pty) Ltd.
Envirotech Corporation
    Envirotech (Pty) Ltd.
    Eimco S.A.
Exxon Corporation
    Esso Standard S.A. (Pty) Ltd.
    Gilbarco South Africa (Pty) Ltd.
    Esso Minerals Africa Inc.
    Esso Chemical (Pty) Ltd.
Ford Motor Company
    Ford Motor Company (S.A.) Ltd.
Franklin Electric
    Franklin Electric S.A. (Pty) Ltd.
Hewlett-Packard Company
    Hewlett-Packard S.A. (Pty) Ltd.
IBM Corporation
    IBM South Africa
Eli Lilly & Company
    Lilly Laboratories (S.A.) (Pty) Ltd.

*Throughout these listings the first line shows the U.S. signatory corporation and the line(s) below each corporation indicate(s) its South African subsidiaries.

Merck & Company, Inc.
    M.S.D. (Pty) Ltd.
Mobil Oil Corporation
    Mobil Oil Southern Africa (Pty) Ltd.
    Mobil Refining Co. (S.A.) (Pty) Ltd.
    Vialit (Proprietary) Limited
    Socony (S.A.) (Pty) Ltd.
    Condor Oil (Pty) Ltd.
    Westchester Insurance Co. (Pty) Ltd.
    S.A. Oil Refinery (Pty) Limited
Minnesota Mining & Manufacturing Company
    3M S.A. (Pty) Ltd.
    Etkinds Management Service (Pty) Ltd.
    Riker Laboratory Africa (Pty) Ltd.
NCR Corporation
    NCR Corporation of S.A. (Pty) Ltd.
Norton Simon, Inc.
    Avis
Schering-Plough Corporation
    Scherag (Pty) Ltd.
Sperry Corporation
    Sperry Rand S.A. (Pty) Ltd.
    Sperry Univac
    Sperry Vickers
Union Carbide Corporation
    Union Carbide Africa & Middle East
    EMSA

Category II. Making Acceptable Progress

Abbott Laboratories
    Abbott Laboratories S.A. (Pty) Ltd.
American Cyanamid Company
    S.A. Cyanamid (Pty) Ltd.
    Lederle Laboratories (Pty) Ltd.
    Shulton Africa Ltd.
    Laminated Industries (Pty) Ltd.
American Express Company
    American Express International, Inc.
American Home Products Corporation
    Ayerst Laboratories (Pty) Ltd.
    Prestige Group South Africa (Pty) Limited
    Whitehall Products S.A. (Pty)
    Wyeth Laboratories (Pty) Limited
American Hospital Supply Corporation
    AHSC/South Africa

Armco Steel Corporation
    Armco (Pty) Ltd.
Borden, Inc.
    Borden (Pty) Ltd.
    Babelegi Processing (Pty) Ltd.
    Resinite (S.A.) (Pty) Ltd.
    D.P.M.C. (Pty) Ltd.
Burroughs Corporation
    Burroughs Machines Ltd.
Caterpillar Tractor Company
    Caterpillar (Africa) (Pty) Ltd.
Champion Spark Plug Company
    Champion Spark Plug Company of South Africa, (Pty) Ltd.
Colgate-Palmolive Company
    The Kendall Company of S.A. (Pty) Ltd.
    S. Weinstein & Company
CPC International
    Corn Products Company (S.A.) (Pty) Ltd.
Dart Industries, Inc.
    Dart Industries (Pty) Ltd.
Deloitte, Haskins, & Sells
    Deloitte, Haskins & Sells (South Africa)
Del Monte Corporation
    South African Preserving Company (Pty) Ltd. Tulback
Donaldson Company, Inc.
    Donaldson Aircleaners, Johannesburg
    Donaldson Aircleaners, Cape Town
ESB Ray-O-Vac
    Willard Africa (Pty) Ltd.
Firestone Tire & Rubber Company
    Firestone S.A. (Pty) Ltd.
FMC Corporation
    FMC South Africa (Pty) Ltd.
General Electric
    South African General Electric Company (Pty) Ltd.
General Motors Corporation
    GMSA (Pty) Ltd.
    GMAC (S.A.) (Pty) Ltd.
The Gillette Company
    Gillette South Africa Ltd.
Goodyear International Corporation
    Goodyear Tire & Rubber Company (S.A.) (Pty) Ltd.
    The Kelly Springfield Tire Company
W.R. Grace & Company
    W.R. Grace (Pty) Ltd.

Heublein, Incorporated

Kentucky Fried Chicken (S.A.) (Pty) Ltd.
Honeywell Incorporated
    Honeywell Automatic (Pty) Ltd.
Hoover Company
INA Corporation
    INA Insurance Company Ltd.
Johnson & Johnson
    Johnson & Johnson (Pty) Ltd.
    Ethnor (Pty) Ltd.
Kellogg Company
    Kellogg Company of S.A. (Pty) Ltd.
Kennecott Copper Corporation
    Tisand (Pty) Ltd.
    Richards Bay Iron & Titanium (Pty) Ltd.
    Carborundum
Eli Lilly & Company
    Elizabeth Arden (S.A.) (Pty) Ltd.
Masonite Corporation
    Masonite (Africa) Ltd.
    Magnolia Plantations (Pty) Ltd.
McGraw-Hill Incorporated
    McGraw-Hill Book Company (S.A.) (Pty)
Merck & Company, Inc.
    Baltimore Aircoil Company S.A. (Pty) Ltd.
Monsanto Company
    Monsanto South Africa (Pty) Ltd. (MOSAF)
Motorola Inc.
    Motorola S.A. (Pty) Ltd.
The Nalco Chemical Company
    Anikem (Pty) Ltd.
A.C. Nielsen International, Inc.
    A.C. Nielsen Company (Pty) Ltd.
Olin Corporation
    Lion Chemicals Pty. Ltd.
    Aquachlor Pty. Ltd.
Otis Elevator Company
    Otis Elevator Company Ltd.
The Parker Pen Company
    The Parker Pen (Pty) Ltd.-R.S.A.
Pfizer, Inc.
    Pfizer (Pty) Ltd.
    Pfizer Laboratories (Pty) Ltd.
Phillips Chemical Company
    Phillips Carbon Black (Pty) Ltd.
Reader's Digest Association, Inc.
    The Reader's Digest Association South Africa (Pty) Ltd.   99

Rexnord, Inc.
    Nordberg Mfg. Company (S.A.) (Pty) Ltd.
Richardson-Merrell, Inc.
    R.M. Pharmaceuticals (Pty) Limited S.A.
Rohm & Haas Company
    Rohm & Haas (S.A.) (Pty) Ltd.
Simplicity Pattern Company, Inc.
    Simplicity Patterns (S.A.) (Pty) Ltd.
The Singer Company
    Singer S.A. (Pty) Ltd.
Smith Kline
    Smith Kline & French (Pty) Ltd.
Squibb Corporation
    Squibb Laboratories (Pty) Ltd.
    Beech-Nut Life Savers Ltd.
    SkyChef (Pty) Ltd.
Sterling Drug Incorporated
    Sterling Drug S.A. (Pty) Ltd.
The Trane Company
    Trane Southern Africa (Pty) Ltd.
TRW, Incorporated
Union Carbide Corporation
    Union Carbide Africa & Middle East Inc.
    UCAR Minerals Corporation
    UCAR Chrome Corporation
    Union Carbide South Africa (Pty) Ltd.
    Tubatse Ferrochrome (Pty) Ltd.
Uniroyal, Incorporated
    Uniroyal (Pty) Ltd.
The Upjohn Company
    Upjohn (Pty) Ltd.
    Asgrow Seed Company
Warner-Lambert Company
    Chamberlain's (Pty) Ltd.
    Parke-Davis Laboratories (Pty) Ltd.
Westinghouse Electric Corporation
    Ottermill S.A. (Pty) Ltd.
Wilbur-Ellis Company
    Wilbur-Ellis Company (Pty) Ltd.
Xerox Corporation
    Rank Xerox (Pty) Ltd.

Category III. Needs to Become More Active
AFIA Worldwide Insurance
Monarch South Africa Insurance Co. Ltd.

Butterick Fashion Marketing Co.
    Butterick Fashion Marketing Company S.A. (Pty) Ltd.
Carnation Company
    Carnation Foods (Pty) Ltd.
Federal-Mogul Corporation
    Femo (Pty) Ltd.
Ferro Corp.
    Ferro Industrial Products (Pty) Ltd.
International Harvester Co.
    International Harvester Company of S.A.
    Soilmaster Limited
International Minerals & Chemicals Corp.
    Lavino South Africa (Pty) Ltd.
The Interpublic Group of Companies, Inc.
    Metropolitan Advertising Co. (Pty) Ltd.
    Campbell-Ewald (Pty) Ltd.
    McCann-Erickson S.A. (Pty) Ltd.
Tampax, Inc.
    Tampax S.A. (Pty) Ltd.

Category IV. Inadequate Report
Pan American World Airways Inc.
Engelhard Minerals & Chemicals Corporation

Category V. Submitting First Report
American International Group
    American International Insurance Company Ltd.
Automated Building Components, Inc.
    Automated Building Components S.A. (Pty) Ltd.
Borg-Warner Corporation
    Borg-Warner-Axle Division
    Borg-Warner-Parts & Service Division
Bristol-Myers Company
    B-M Group (Pty) Ltd.
Celanese Corporation
    Stein Hall S.A. (Pty) Ltd.
Measurex Corporation
    Measurex S.A. (Pty) Ltd.
Nashua Corporation
Sentry Insurance Mutual Company (U.S.)
    Permanent Life-Assurance Company-S.A.

Category VI. Endorsers
(With no employees)
Bethlehem Steel Corporation
Bulova Watch Company, Inc.

Walter E. Heller Overseas Corporation
Nabisco Incorporated
Oshkosh Truck Corporation
Rockwell International Corporation
White Motor Corporation

(Chose not to report because of small number of employees)
Twin Disk (8 employees)
E.I. DuPont De Nemours & Company (3 employees)
Cummins Engine Company, Inc. (5 employees)

Category VII. New Signatories
The Badger Company, Inc.
Dow Chemical Company
Farrell Lines, Inc.
John Fluke Manufacturing Company, Inc.
Fluor, Inc.
Grolier, Inc.
GAF Corporation
The Gates Rubber Company
J. Gerber & Company
Hyster Company
Johnson Control International, Inc.
Mine Safety Appliances Company
North Carolina National Bank
Pennwalt Corporation
International Standard Brand, Inc.
J. Walter Thompson
Tokheim Corporation

Category VIII. Signatories Who Did Not Report
Bundy Corporation
Crown Cork & Seal Company, Inc.
Cutler-Hammer, Inc.
Gardner-Denver Company
ITT
Norton Company
Phelps Dodge Corporation
Revlon
Schering-Plough Corporation
Scholl Company

Category IX. Signatory Headquartered Outside the U.S.
The East Asiatic Company (S.A.) (Pty) Ltd.

***Category X. U.S. Businesses in South Africa (According
to American Consulate General, Johannesburg) Who Are
Not Signatories to The Sullivan Principles***

ABS Worldwide Technical Services, Inc.
Addressograph-Multigraph Corporation
Air Express International Corporation
Alcon Universal Ltd.
Allegheny Ludlum Industries, Inc.
Allis Chalmers Corporation
Allied Kelite Chemicals, Inc.
A.M. International, Inc.
American Air Filter Company, Inc.
Amchem Products, Inc.
American Airlines
American Broadcasting Company
American Bureau of Shipping
Amrho International SA
Anderson Clayton & Company
Applied Power, Inc.
Arthur Andersen & Company
Arthur Young & Co.
Associated Metals & Minerals Corporation
The Associated Press
Balkinds Agencies Pty. Ltd.
Bausch & Lomb, Inc.
Baxter Laboratories, Inc.
BBDO International, Inc.
Bechtel Corporation
Beckman Instruments, Inc.
Bell & Howell Company
Berkshire International Corporation
Black Clawson Overseas
The Black & Decker Manufacturing Company
Blue Bell, Inc.
The Boeing Company
Buckman Laboratories, Inc.
Bucyrus-Erie Company
Carrier Corporation
Cascade Corporation
J.I. Case International
CBS International, Inc.
CBS News
Chesebrough-Pond's, Inc.
Chicago Bridge & Iron Company
Chicago Pneumatic Tool Company
Christian Science Monitor

Chrysler Corporation
Cinema International Corporation N.V.
Clark International
The Coca-Cola Company
Columbus McKinnon Corporation
Computer Sciences Corporation
Continental Grain Company
Dames & Moore
D'Arcy-MacManus & Masius Worldwide, Inc.
DHJ Industries, Inc.
Diners Club, Inc.
Diversey Corporation
Dow Corning Corporation
Dresser Industries, Inc.
Dubois International
Dun & Bradstreet International Ltd.
Eaton Corporation
Echlin Manufacturing Company
Expresas Sudamericana Consolidadas S.A.
Fenix & Scisson, Inc.
First National Bank of Boston
Foster Wheeler Corporation
Fuller Company/GATX
Gamlen Chemical Corporation
General Tire & Rubber Company
Geosource, Inc.
Gilbert & Baker Mfg. Co.
Harnischfeger Corporation
Harper Robinson, Inc.
Heinemann Electric Company
Hussman International, Inc.
IMS International, Inc.
Ingersoll-Rand Company
International Flavors & Fragrances, Inc.
International Playtex, Inc.
S.C. Johnson & Son, Inc.
Joy Manufacturing Co.
Kimberly-Clark Corporation
Koehring Company
L & M Radiator, Inc.
Leco Corp.
Loctite Corp.
The Los Angeles Times
Lubrizol Corp.
Lykes Brothers Steamship Company, Inc.

M&T Chemicals, Inc.

Macmillan, Inc.
Mallory International
Maremont Corporation
Marriott Corporation
Max Factor & Company
MDS Executive Headquarters
Memorex Corporation
Metro-Goldwyn Mayer International, Inc.
George J. Meyer Manufacturing
Miles Laboratories, Inc.
Moore McCormack Lines, Inc.
Muller & Phipps International Corp.
National Broadcasting Company
National Chemsearch Corporation
National Standard Company
National Starch & Chemical Corp.
National Utility Service, Inc.
Newmont Mining Corp.
Newsweek, Inc.
The New York Times
Oak Technology, Inc.
Owens-Corning Fiberglass Corporation
Pacific Oilseeds, Inc.
Parker Hannifin Corporation
Pepsico International Purchase
Perkin-Elmer Corporation
C.J. Petrow & Co.
PHH Group Inc.
Pizza Inn
Precision Valve Corp.
Preformed Line Products Company
Preload Engineering Corp.
Premix Asphalt Company
Price Waterhouse & Company
Ramsey Engineering Company
Reed Mining Tool, Inc.
Rheem International, Inc.
Robbin Company
H.H. Robertson Co.
A.H. Robins Co., Inc.
Charles St. Thomas Group
G.D. Searle Co.
Sedco, Inc.
Sperry Remington
Standard Pressed Steel Co.
The Stanley Works

Stauffer Chemical Co.
Stratoflex (Pty) Ltd.
Sybron Corp.
Tantatex Chemical Corp.
Technicon Corp.
Tedd McKune Investment Company (Pty) Ltd.
Tenneco International, Inc.
Texas Gulf, Inc.
Time, Inc.
Timken Co.
Trans World Airlines, Inc.
20th Century-Fox International Corp.
United Artists Corp.
United States Filter Corporation
United States Gypsum Company
United States Industries
US. News & World Report
U.S. Steel Corp.
UPI, Inc.
Utah International, Inc.
Valeron Corp.
Valvoline Oil Co.
Van Dusen Air, Inc.
Warner Brothers International, Inc.
The Washington Post Co.
West Point Pepperell
Western Airlines, Inc.
Western International Hotel
Whinney Murray Ernst & Ernst

APPENDIX II

RESOLUTION ON THE SULLIVAN PRINCIPLES AND ECONOMIC DISENGAGEMENT

International Freedom Mobilization
Summit Conference of Black Religious Leaders
On Apartheid
New York, April 17-19, 1979

Whereas, apartheid has been universally and properly identified as a crime against humanity and,

Whereas, United States economic investment and the hundreds of United States multinational corporations and banks serve to maintain and strengthen the apartheid structure of South Africa and,

Whereas, numerous voices of our African brothers and sisters have called on us to join in solidarity with their struggle by working to terminate United States economic, political, military and cultural collaboration with the racist apartheid regime and,

Whereas, the deaths of so many of our people continue, be it from daily death of starvation and slave wages or from the episodic mass slaughterings as at Sharpeville in 1960 and at Soweto on June 16, 1976;

We Resolve that the Sullivan Principles, though well-intentioned, are no longer sufficient and that the very presence of United States corporations in South Africa serves to legitimize the apartheid system of white supremacy;

Further, we resolve to work towards total United States economic, political, military, cultural and diplomatic disengagement from South Africa until the white supremacist government with its policy of racism, brutality and exploitation is ended.

RESOLUTION IN SUPPORT OF THE AFRICAN NATIONAL CONGRESS (ANC)

Whereas, the history of the struggle of the people of South Africa has been one continuous battle against the demonic regime and human exploitation; and,

Whereas, this struggle has been spearheaded by the African National Congress since 1912; and,

Whereas, the people of South Africa have tried every peaceful and rational means of changing the hearts and minds of the white minority; and,

Whereas, the world community in recognition of this peaceful attempt by the A.N.C. conferred upon its president, the honorable Chief Albert Luthuli, himself a Christian minister, the Nobel Peace Prize in 1961 for his efforts; and,

Whereas, the Christian Church has spoken out against the evils of the regime and still the holocaust against Blacks continues and has escalated; and,

Whereas, the World Council of Churches has gone on record in support of the liberation movements;

Be It Resolved that this Summit Conference of Black Religious Leaders on Apartheid declare its unequivocal support of the national liberation struggle waged by the South African people under the leadership of the African National Congress.

APPENDIX III

EXCERPTS FROM: FOREIGN INVESTMENT IN SOUTH AFRICA

African National Congress
November 30, 1977

The African National Congress has always recognised and accepted that the main burden and responsibility for the liberation struggle rests upon the South African people. We believe however that international action has a significant role to play, and that as the liberation movement of the South African people, we have a duty and the right to indicate what actions beyond our country's borders further the liberation struggle, and what methods may hamper it . . .

International support for the apartheid system—military, economic and political—is quite considerable. The erosion and withdrawal of this support can and will shorten our struggle and diminish the price paid for freedom in the suffering of our people. There is a contradiction between the professed and oft-stated condemnation of apartheid and the concrete links that are maintained with and sustain the apartheid system. At the very least the South African people expect, and ask, that these links be now severed.

The African National Congress has therefore renewed its call for the total isolation of the apartheid regime, and in particular to the ending of those connections which buttress and give strength to the apartheid system. A priority area for action is in preventing the further export of capital to South Africa. The apartheid economy is now more dependent than ever before upon the inflow of foreign capital. Increasingly, foreign investment is required to finance balance of payments deficits, to maintain capital growth programmes, and to service the growing foreign debt. Within the decade since 1966 the annual contribution of foreign capital (net inflow) to the gross domestic fixed investment rose from 7.1% to over 25%; and in the same period direct and indirect foreign investment in South Africa more than doubled, and by the end of 1973 had reached over Rands 10,380 million . . .

109

Technology is the one completely irreplaceable item which the South African racists obtain via foreign investment. Every piece of new technology has potential repressive and manipulative applications—from the computerised enforcement of the pass laws (the single biggest burden on black South Africans) to communications technology taking apartheid propaganda to Blacks. Foreign technology has increased the efficiency of the political police (the Special Branch and BOSS) in their surveillance of the peoples' organizations.

It has enabled the apartheid regime to build up a vast local armaments industry in anticipation of a possible arms embargo, with planes, missiles, ships and vehicles as well as weapons being produced in South Africa under licence. Foreign technology has made South Africa a nuclear power and given Vorster the capacity to threaten and intimidate the neighbouring countries. As the intervention in Zimbabwe, the continued illegal occupation of Namibia, and the invasion of Angola testify, the Pretoria regime is now a threat to peace and security. It is able to maintain this threat because of the availability of technology from abroad . . .

The African National Congress does not underestimate the practical difficulties, nor do we refuse to acknowledge the problems likely to be caused in certain domestic economies by severance of links with apartheid. In our view, however, these need to be seen against the unplanned disruption that must inevitably come in the course of a prolonged armed struggle in South Africa.

The main obstacle to disengagement today is not the practical one, but rather lies in the lack of will to withdraw—in the short-sighted view that concerns itself only with the comparatively high rate of return from investment in apartheid. . .

The improvement of working conditions can never be accepted as substitutes for liberation. Slavery was and can never be made acceptable by providing good food and comfortable slave quarters . . .

Foreign investors have played a leading role in creating and establishing the apartheid institutions and structures within the economy, and have continued to strengthen racism in our country. There is nothing in their record of action inside South Africa (as distinct from rhetoric) which supports the proposition that they are now about to make a 180° turn and begin to undo the racist and exploitative system they have helped establish.

Foreign companies have invested in South Africa because it has been profitable to do so. Their investment has been particularly profitable because of the migratory labour system, influx control, the pass laws, non-recognition of trade unions, and the repressive police system which has been repeatedly used to intimidate and attack workers. No protest has come from foreign companies about these, nor have they done anything even within the limited scope legally possible to assist their workers in these fields.

In present conditions, the laws and attitude of the regime are such, that even if foreign companies wished to effect radical changes they would be unable to do so to any significant extent, even in the limited field of employment. Outside of this, the companies do not have the power to alter the major dimensions of racism and the apartheid system.

They cannot democratize the political system. They cannot stop the police from harassing, torturing, murdering, and shooting our people. They cannot end the pass laws, residential segregation, Bantu Education. They cannot re-distribute 87% of the land abrogated by whites to the black population. Even within their own factories, there is only a limited degree to which they can take measures to which either their white employees or the regime object.

Liberation entails the transfer of power to the majority of the population on the basis of one person one vote; land for all; national control over the commanding heights of the economy; and an end to exploitation . . .

The Liberation Movement's View on Foreign Investment:

It should be noted that the call for the international isolation of South Africa has come initially from the people of South Africa. *No organization, save those that accept apartheid and work within the system, has supported continued foreign investment in the apartheid economy.*

The African National Congress here expresses the overwhelming mass of the oppressed people in asking:

1. *For an immediate ban on all further foreign investment* in

South Africa to be imposed by each government, without waiting for agreement on simultaneous international actions.

2. *For the withdrawal of all existing investment in South Africa.* This should not be a symbolic gesture, with the reality of foreign investment continuing by selling to a South African owned company and allowing it to use under licence the processes and products involved.

3. *For the denial of all modern technology to the South African economy.* No new licences should be granted to companies operating in South Africa, and existing licences, patents and related agreements should be revoked.

These three positions do not—obviously—constitute the sum total of the ANC's views on international pressures on the South African regime. We believe, however, that implementation of these measures in regard to foreign investment would make a significant contribution towards eradicating racism in South Africa and furthering the liberation of our country.

APPENDIX IV

AMPLIFIED GUIDELINES TO SOUTH AFRICAN STATEMENT OF PRINCIPLES

Principle I Non-segregation of the races in all eating, comfort and work facilities.

Each signator of the Statement of Principles will proceed immediately to:
- Eliminate all vestiges of racial discrimination.
- Remove all race designation signs.
- Desegregate all eating, comfort and work facilities.

Principle II Equal and fair employment practices for all employees.

Each signator of the Statement of Principles will proceed immediately to:
- Implement equal and fair terms and conditions of employment.
- Provide non-discriminatory eligiblity for benefit plans.
- Establish an appropriate comprehensive procedure for handling and resolving individual employee complaints.
- Support the elimination of all industrial racial discriminatory laws which impede the implementation of equal and fair terms and conditions of employment, such as abolition of job reservations, job fragmentation, and apprenticeship restrictions for Blacks and other non-whites.
- Support the elimination of discrimination against the rights of Blacks to form or belong to government registered unions, and acknowledge generally the right of Black workers to form their own union or be represented by trade unions where unions already exist.

Principle III Equal pay for all employees doing equal or comparable work for the same period of time.

Each signator of the Statement of Principles will proceed immediately to:
- Design and implement a wage and salary administration plan which is applied equally to all employees regardless of race who are performing equal or comparable work.
- Ensure an equitable system of job classifications, including a

113

review of the distinction between hourly and salaried classifications.

• Determine whether upgrading of personnel and/or jobs in the lower echelons is needed, and if so, implement programs to accomplish this objective expeditiously.

• Assign equitable wage and salary ranges, the minimum of these to be well above the appropriate local minimum economic living level.

Principle IV Initiation of and development of training programs that will prepare, in substantial numbers, Blacks and other non-whites for supervisory, administrative, clerical and technical jobs.

Each signator of the Statement of Principles will proceed immediately to:

• Determine employee training needs and capabilities, and identify employees with potential for further advancement.

• Take advantage of existing outside training resources and activities, such as exchange programs, technical colleges, vocational schools, continuation classes, supervisory courses and similar institutions or programs.

• Support the development of outside training facilities individually or collectively, including technical centers, professional training exposure, correspondence and extension courses, as appropriate, for extensive training outreach.

• Initiate and expand inside training programs and facilities.

Principle V Increasing the number of Blacks and other non-whites in management and supervisory positions.

Each signator of the Statement of Principles will proceed immediately to:

• Identify, actively recruit, train and develop a sufficient and significant number of Blacks and other non-whites to assure that as quickly as possible there will be appropriate representation of Blacks and other non-whites in the management group of each company at all levels of operations.

• Establish management development programs for Blacks and other non-whites, as appropriate, and improve existing programs and facilities for developing management skills of Blacks and other non-whites.

• Identify and channel high management potential Blacks and other non-white employees into management development programs.

114   **Principle VI** Improving the quality of employees' lives outside

the work environment in such areas as housing, transportation, schooling, recreation and health facilities.

Each signator of the Statement of Principles will proceed immediately to:
• Evaluate existing and/or develop programs, as appropriate, to address the specific needs of Black and other non-white employees in the areas of housing, health care, transportation and recreation.
• Evaluate methods for utilizing existing, expanded or newly established in-house medical facilities or other medical programs to improve medical care for all non-whites and their dependents.
• Participate in the development of programs that address the educational needs of employees, their dependents and the local community. Both individual and collective programs should be considered, including such activities as literacy education, business training, direct assistance to local schools, contributions and scholarships.
• Support changes in influx control laws to provide for the right of Black migrant workers to normal family life.
• Increase utilization of and assist in the development of Black and non-white-owned and operated business enterprises including distributors, suppliers of goods and services and manufacturers.
• With all the foregoing in mind, it is the objective of the companies to involve and assist in the education and training of large and telling numbers of Blacks and other non-whites as quickly as possible. The ultimate impact of this effort is intended to be of massive proportion, reaching millions.

Periodic Reporting

The signator companies of the Statement of Principles will proceed immediately to:
• Utilize a standard format to report their progress to Dr. Sullivan through the independent administrative unit which he has established on a 6-month basis.
• Ensure periodic reports on the progress that has been accomplished on the implementation of these principles.

Reproduced from "Amplified Guidelines to South African Statement of Principles," Reverend Leon H. Sullivan, May 1, 1979.

BIBLIOGRAPHY
AND RESOURCES

Further Reading on U.S. Economic Involvement in South Africa:

American Friends Service Committee. *Action Guide on Southern Africa.* Philadelphia, American Friends Service Committee, 1976.

Corporate Data Exchange (Beate Klein, Research Director). *U.S. Bank Loans to South Africa.* New York, Corporate Data Exchange, 1978.

Corporate Data Exchange (Beate Klein, Project Director). *Bank Loans to South Africa, 1972-1978. (Notes and Documents* no. 5/79) New York, United Nations Centre Against Apartheid, May 1979.

Ruth First, Jonathan Steele, and Christabel Gurney. *The South African Connection: Western Investment in Apartheid.* Middlesex, England, Penguin Books, 1973.

Julian R. Friedman. *Basic Facts on the Republic of South Africa and the Policy of Apartheid. (Notes and Documents* no. 8/77/Rev. 1) New York, United Nations Centre Against Apartheid, October 1978.

Lawrence Litvak, Robert DeGrasse, and Kathleen McTigue. *South Africa: Foreign Investment and Apartheid.* Washington, D.C., Institute for Policy Studies, 1978.

Bernard M. Magubane. *The Political Economy of Race and Class in South Africa.* New York, Monthly Review Press, 1979.

Desaix Myers III, with Kenneth Propp, David Hauck, and David M. Liff. *U.S. Business in South Africa: The Economic, Political, and Moral Issues.* Bloomington, Indiana University Press, 1980.

Barbara Rogers. *White Wealth and Black Poverty: American Investments in Southern Africa.* Westport, Connecticut, Greenwood Press, 1976.

Elizabeth Schmidt. "The Sullivan Principles: Decoding Corporate Camouflage." Washington, D.C., Institute for Policy Studies, 1979.

Ann and Neva Seidman. *South Africa and U.S. Multinational Corporations.* Westport, Connecticut, Lawrence Hill & Co., 1977.

Ann Seidman and Neva Makgetla. *Transnational Corporations and the South African Military-Industrial Complex.* (*Notes and Documents* no. 24/79) New York, United Nations Centre Against Apartheid, September 1979.

South Africa Catalyst Project. *Anti-Apartheid Organizing on Campus and Beyond.* Palo Alto, California, South Africa Catalyst Project, 1979.

U.S. Congress, Senate Committee on Foreign Relations, Subcommittee on African Affairs. *U.S. Corporate Interests in Africa.* Washington, D.C., U.S. Government Printing Office, 1978.

Periodicals Pertaining to Southern Africa

Africa News (weekly)
P.O. Box 3851
Durham, North Carolina 27702

Africa Today (quarterly)
c/o Graduate School of International Studies
University of Denver
Denver, Colorado 80208

Facts and Reports (bi-weekly)
Holland Committee on Southern Africa
Da Costastraat 88
Amsterdam, The Netherlands

Journal of Southern African Affairs (quarterly)
Art/Sociology Building, Room #4133
University of Maryland
College Park, Maryland 20742

Southern Africa (monthly)
17 West 17th Street
New York, New York 10011

UFAHAMU
African Activists Association
African Studies Center
University of California
Los Angeles, California 90024

Organizations Concerned with Southern Africa Support Work

American Committee on Africa/The Africa Fund
198 Broadway, Room #402
New York, New York 10038
(212) 962-1210

American Friends Service Committee
Southern Africa Program
1501 Cherry Street
Philadelphia, Pennsylvania 19102
(215) 241-7000

Committee to Oppose Bank Loans to South Africa
198 Broadway, Room #402
New York, New York 10038
(212) 962-1210

Interfaith Center on Corporate Responsibility
475 Riverside Drive, Room #566
New York, New York 10027
(212) 870-2295

International Defense and Aid Fund for Southern Africa
P.O. Box 17
Cambridge, Massachusetts 02138
(617) 495-4940

Liberation Support Movement Information Center
P.O. Box 2077
Oakland, California 94604
(415) 655-5311

New World Resource Center
1476 West Irving Park Road
Chicago, Illinois 60613
(312) 348-3370

Southern Africa Media Center, California Newsreel
630 Natoma Street
San Francisco, California 94103
(415) 621-6196

TransAfrica
1325 18th Street N.W.
Washington, D.C. 20036
(202) 223-9666

United Nations Centre Against Apartheid
Notes and Documents, Room #2775
United Nations Plaza
New York, New York 10017
(212) 754-6674

Washington Office on Africa
110 Maryland Avenue, N.E.
Washington, D.C. 20002
(202) 546-7961

FOOTNOTES

1. Davis, David. *African Workers and Apartheid*. London, International Defence and Aid Fund, March 1978, p. 5.

2. Murphy, Caryle. "Pass System: Daily Affront to Black South Africans," *Washington Post,* August 23, 1979.

3. U.S. House of Representatives, Committee on International Relations, Subcommittees on Africa and on International Economic Policy and Trade. *United States Private Investment in South Africa.* Hearings. Washington, D.C., U.S. Government Printing Office, 1978, p. 172.

4. *A Survey of Race Relations in South Africa 1978.* Johannesburg, South African Institute of Race Relations, 1979, p. 141.

   Corporate Information Center. *Church Investments, Corporations, and South Africa.* New York, Friendship Press, 1973, p. 9.

   Seidman, Ann and Neva. *South Africa and U.S. Multinational Corporations.* Westport, Connecticut, Lawrence Hill & Co., 1977, p. 80.

5. American Friends Service Committee. *Southern Africa Must Be Free.* Philadelphia, American Friends Service Committee, 1978, p. 14.

6. Friedman, Julian R. *Basic Facts on the Republic of South Africa and the Policy of Apartheid.* (Notes and Documents no. 8/77/Rev. 1) New York, United Nations Centre Against Apartheid, October 1978, pp. 21, 51.

7. Harrell, Joan and Rothmyer, Karen. "South Africa Fact Sheet." New York, The Africa Fund, #1-79, p. 3.

8. Ibid., p. 2.

9. Friedman, op. cit., pp. 19-20.

10. U.S. House of Representatives, Committee on International Relations, Subcommittee on International Organizations. *Human Rights Conditions in Selected Countries and the U.S. Response.* Branaman, Brenda. "Human Rights Conditions in South Africa," p. 249.

11. Amnesty International. *Political Imprisonment in South Africa.* London, Amnesty International, 1978, p. 21.

12. Ibid., p. 33.

13. Ibid., p. 40.

14. Trewhitt, Henry L. "Vorster Says U.S. Threats Predated His Crackdown," *The Sun,* October 24, 1977.

15. Amnesty International, op. cit., p. 99; "U.S. Group to Build School in Soweto," *The Sun,* October 4, 1979.

16. Amnesty International, op. cit., p. 39; Harrell and Rothmyer, op. cit., p. 4.

17. "A South African Black Dies, Possibly Tortured," *New York Times,* July 21, 1978, p. 2.

18. Seidman, Ann and Makgetla, Neva. *Transnational Corporations and the South African Military-Industrial Complex.* (Notes and Documents no. 24/79) New York, United Nations Centre Against Apartheid, September 1979, pp. 1-2.

The Military Balance 1975-76. London, International Institute for Strategic Studies, 1975, p. 77.

The Military Balance 1979-80. London, International Institute for Strategic Studies, 1979, p. 95.

19. Myers, Desaix, III. *Business and Labor in South Africa.* Washington, D.C., Investor Responsibility Research Center, May 1979, p. 41; Harrell and Rothmyer, op. cit., p. 2.

20. Kahn, E.J., Jr. "Annals of International Trade," *New Yorker,* May 14, 1979, p. 137.

21. Quoted in: "Statements Concerning Labour Codes," *South African Outlook,* vol. 109, no. 1295, May 1979, p. 77.

22. Resolutions of the International Freedom Mobilization Summit Conference of Black Religious Leaders on Apartheid. New York, New York, April 17-19, 1979.

23. Walker, Rev. Wyatt Tee. "Where Do We Go From Here," International Freedom Mobilization Summit Conference, op. cit., April 19, 1979, p. 8.

24. Trescott, Jacqueline. "Principles & Palates," *Washington Post,* November 30, 1979, p. C3.

25. Myers, op. cit., p. 84.

26. Kahn, op. cit., p. 140.

27. *Third Report on the Signatory Companies to the Sullivan Principles.* Cambridge, Massachusetts, Arthur D. Little Co., Inc., October 15, 1979, p. 4.

28. Nickel, Herman. "The Case for Doing Business in South Africa," *Fortune,* June 19, 1978, p. 72; Myers, op. cit., pp. 87-88.

29. Bawtree, Victoria, ed. "Apartheid," *Ideas and Action.* Rome, Food and Agriculture Organization of the United Nations, 1978, p. 9.

30. "Apartheid for 'Industrial Peace'." Washington, D.C., Washington Office on Africa, 1979, pp. 2-3.

31. *First Report on the Signatory Companies to the Sullivan Principles.* Cambridge, Massachusetts, Arthur D. Little Co., Inc., November 17, 1978, Table 13; Myers, op. cit., p. 99.

121

32. *Bulletin of Statistics,* vol. 13, no. 3. Republic of South Africa, Department of Statistics, September 1979, p. 2.4, 2.7: Davis, David. op. cit., p. 20.

33. Davis, Jennifer. "Too Little, Too Late, the U.S. Corporation Employment Manifesto for South Africa." New York, The Africa Fund, April 1977, p. 2.

34. Myers, op. cit., p. 97; "Ford Motor Co.," Company Report. Washington, D.C., Investor Responsibility Research Center, February 1980, pp. 2-3.

35. "General Motors Corp.," Company Report. Washington, D.C., Investor Responsibility Research Center, February 1980, p. 2.

36. "Masonite Corp.," Company Report. Washington, D.C., Investor Responsibility Research Center, February 1980, pp. 2, 6.

37. Ellen Ruppert, Consultant for the Arthur D. Little Co., Inc. Telephone interview, December 7, 1979.

38. Myers, op. cit., p. 73.

39. Liff, David M. *The Computer and Electronics Industry in South Africa.* Washington, D.C., Investor Responsibility Research Center, March 1979, pp. 13, 15.

40. Ibid., p. 16.

41. Ruppert, op. cit.

42. Ibid.

43. "Ford Motor Co.," Company Report, op. cit., p. 15; "Sullivan Principles Summary Report" for Union Carbide and Exxon for the period ending June 30, 1978, pp. 9-10.

44. "Control Data Corp.," Company Report. Washington, D.C., Investor Responsibility Research Center, January 1980, pp. 7, 8, 10, 15.

45. "Honeywell, Inc.," Company Report. Washington, D.C., Investor Responsibility Research Center, November 1979, pp. 4, 5.

46. Ibid., p. 10.

47. U.S. House of Representatives, Committee on International Relations, Subcommittee on International Organizations, op. cit., p. 247.

48. Johannesburg Advice Office of the Black Sash. "Emergency Report." November 1979, p. 2.

49. "Sullivan Principles Summary Report" for Ford Motor Co. for the period ending June 30, 1978, p. 11.

50. Myers, op. cit., p. 92.

51. Sullivan, Rev. Leon H. "Amplified Guidelines to South African Statement of Principles." May 1, 1979, p. 1.

52. *Rand Daily Mail,* December 19, 1979; Johnny Carson, Staff

Director of the House Subcommittee on Africa. Report on a memo from the Africa Bureau, U.S. Department of State.

53. Quoted in: "U.S. Business in South Africa: Voices for Withdrawal." New York, The Africa Fund, #1-78, p. 4.

54. Quoted in: Dahm, Father Charles. "The Case Against Investment in South Africa." New York, Interfaith Center on Corporate Respnsibility, May 1979, p. 3C.

55. Senator Paul Tsongas. Press briefing on his trip to South Africa. Washington, D.C., January 15, 1980.

56. African National Congress. "Submission on the Question of Foreign Investment in South Africa," November 30, 1977, p. 15.

57. Quoted in: "U.S. Business in South Africa: Voices for Withdrawal," op. cit., p. 4.

58. Propp, Kenneth and Myers, Desaix, III. *The Motor Industry in South Africa.* Washington, D.C., Investor Responsibility Research Center, February 1979, p. 6.

59. Myers, op. cit., p. 43.

60. Report of Dennis Brutus, participant in the Ford Foundation-sponsored conference at Princeton University where the statement was made. Interview, Cleveland, Ohio, October 13, 1979.

61. Rev. Leon H. Sullivan, National Press Club, Washington, D.C., October 18, 1979.

62. Daniel W. Purnell, Executive Director, International Council for Equality of Opportunity Principles. Telephone interview, January 21, 1980.

63. The Edna McConnell Clark Foundation, *Annual Report 1979.*

64. Ibid.; The Edna McConnell Clark Foundation, "IRS Statement of Tax Exempt Organizations for Fiscal Year End September 30, 1978"; *The Foundation Center Source Book,* The Foundation Center, Washington, D.C.

65. Rev. Leon H. Sullivan, National Press Club, Washington, D.C., October 18, 1979.

66. Berney, Louis and Snider, Steve. "Space Research Corp.: Its Tough Survival Struggle," *Rutland Herald,* December 12, 1978; Telephone interview with Jean de Valpine, May 27, 1980.

67. Hemingway, Sam and Malone, William Scott. "S. Africa Part-Owner of Arms Firm," *Burlington Free Press,* March 14, 1980.

68. Hemingway, Sam and Malone, William Scott. "CIA Knew Space Research was Ready to Sell Advanced Artillery Shells to S. Africa," *Burlington Free Press,* January 6, 1980.

69. Ibid.

70. Ibid.

71. Ibid.; "Hot Shells—U.S. Arms for South Africa," WGBH-T.V., Boston January 16, 1980.

72. Bradlee, Ben. "Vermont Firm Allegedly Sold Arms Illegally to S. Africa," *Boston Globe,* August 26, 1978.

73. Hemingway, Sam and Malone, William Scott. "South Africa Arms Saga: Immunity for One," *Burlington Free Press,* July 11, 1979.

74. Sullivan, Rev. Leon H. "Amplified Guidelines to South African Statement of Principles," op. cit., p. 1.

75. Rev. Leon H. Sullivan. Interview with Patricia Brett, PACIFICA Radio, November 14, 1979.

76. Davis, Jennifer. "US Dollars in South Africa: Context and Consequence." New York, The Africa Fund, February 1978, p. 3.

77. U.S. Senate, Committee on Foreign Relations, Subcommittee on African Affairs. *U.S. Corporate Interests in Africa.* Report. Washington, D.C., U.S. Government Printing Office, 1978, pp. 12-13.

78. Rothmyer, Karen. *U.S. Motor Industry in South Africa: Ford, General Motors and Chrysler.* New York, The Africa Fund, January 1979, p. 2.

79. Propp and Myers, op. cit., p. 16.

80. Davis, Jennifer. "General Motors in South Africa: Secret Contingency Plans 'In the Event of Civil Unrest.' " New York, The Africa Fund, May 1978, p. 1.

81. Saar, John and Younghusband, Peter. "Jesse Jackson Takes on Pretoria," *Newsweek,* August 13, 1979.

82. Burns, John F. "South African Blacks' Dispute at Ford Motor Reaches to the Heart of Equal Rights Struggle," *New York Times,* December 3, 1979.

83. "Ford Accepts Strikers' Demands," *Africa News,* January 14, 1980 p. 10.

84. "South Africa Bans 3 Blacks From Political Activity," *New York Times,* February 29, 1980.

85. U.S. State Department Cable, January 2, 1980.

86. *Rand Daily Mail,* December 19, 1979.

87. U.S. Senate Department Cable, January 9, 1980.

88. Senator Paul Tsongas. Press briefings on his trip to South Africa. Washington, D.C., January 15, 1980 and January 25, 1980.

89. Congressional press briefing. Washington, D.C., January 22, 1980

90. Rothmyer, Karen and Lowenthal, TerriAnn. "The Sullivan Principles: A Critical Look at the U.S. Corporate Role in South Africa."

New York, The Africa Fund, August 1979, p. 3.

91. Litvak, Lawrence; DeGrasse, Robert; and McTigue, Kathleen. *South Africa: Foreign Investment and Apartheid.* Washington, D.C., Institute for Policy Studies, 1978, p. 50.

92. Ibid.

93. Ibid., p. 51; Leonard, Richard. *Computers in South Africa: a Survey of US Companies.* New York, The Africa Fund, November 1978, pp. 12-14.

94. "Honeywell Inc.," Company Report, op. cit., p. 1.

95. Leonard, op. cit., p. 9.

96. Liff, David M. *The Oil Industry in South Africa.* Washington, D.C., Investor Responsibility Research Center, January 1979, pp. 12-13.

Phillips, Lindsey. "South Africa's Future, 'No Easy Walk to Freedom'," *Working Papers for a New Society,* March/April 1979, p. 33.

97. Liff, *The Oil Industry in South Africa,* op. cit., pp. 16-17.

98. "Fueling Apartheid." New York, Council on Economic Priorities, December 4, 1978, p. 3.

99. Ibid., p. 7.

100. "Honeywell Inc.," Company Report, op. cit., p. 3; "Control Data Corp.," Company Report, op. cit., p. 6.

101. McGloin, David. "Swapping Energy Know-How," *Southern Africa,* vol. XII, no. 7, September 1979, p. 23.

102. Ibid., p. 22.

103. Fluor Proxy Statement 1979. Quoted in: "Fluor: Building Energy Self-Sufficiency in South Africa." New York, The Africa Fund, #5/79, p. 6.

104. Liff, *The Oil Industry in South Africa,* op. cit., p. 6.

105. "Olin Convicted of Violating Arms Embargo," *Southern Africa,* vol. XI, no. 4, May 1978, p. 24; Collins, Dan and Belmont, Jeff. "Olin Keeps its License, Despite Guilty Finding," *New Haven Register,* March 22, 1978.

106. Collins and Belmont, op. cit.

107. Fleishman, Sandra. "No Red Tape for Olin," *New Haven Register,* March 26, 1978.

108. Collins and Belmont, op. cit.

109. Coy, Peter. "Scabs Thwarted at Gun Plant," *Guardian,* October 10, 1979.

110. American Consulate General. "American Firms, Subsidiaries and Affiliates—South Africa." Johannesburg, July 1979. (See Lion

Chemicals (Pty.) Ltd.); The *Third Report on the Signatory Companies to the Sullivan Principles,* op. cit. also lists Aquachlor (Pty.) Ltd. as an Olin subsidiary.

111. Nesbitt, Prexy. *New Strategies for International Action Against Transnational Corporate Collaboration with Apartheid.* (Notes and Documents Sem. 4/79) New York, United Nations Centre Against Apartheid, November 1979, p. 6.

112. *Third Report on the Signatory Companies to the Sullivan Principles,* op. cit., p. 2.

113. "SA Raids into Angola," *Focus,* no. 24. London, International Defence and Aid Fund, September-October 1979, p. 15.

114. "South Africa's Wider War," *Africa News,* November 16, 1979, p. 6.

115. "South Africa, Rhodesia Step Up Attacks," *Southern Africa,* vol. XII, no. 9, November-December 1979, p. 2.

116. *Activities of Transnational Corporations in Southern Africa: Impact on Financial and Social Structures.* (no. E/C.10/39) New York, United Nations Economic and Social Council, March 16, 1978, p. 24.

Corporate Data Exchange. *U.S. Bank Loans to South Africa.* New York, Corporate Data Exchange, Inc., 1978, p. 6.

117. Corporate Data Exchange. *Bank Loans to South Africa, 1972-1978.* (Notes and Documents no. 5/79) New York, United Nations Centre Against Apartheid, May 1979, p. 8.

118. "Citicorp," Company Report. Washington, D.C., Investor Responsibility Research Center, February 1980, p. 1; "Financing Apartheid—Citibank in South Africa." New York, Interfaith Center on Corporate Responsibility, March 1980, p. 4.

119. "Financing Apartheid—Citibank in South Africa," op. cit., pp. 3-5.

120. Ibid., p. 4.

121. "Citicorp," op. cit., p. 3.

122. "Financing Apartheid—Citibank in South Africa," op. cit., p. 6.

123. "Citicorp," op. cit., p. 4.

124. "Financing Apartheid—Citibank in South Africa," op. cit., p. 3.

125. Ibid., p. 2.

126. "Citicorp," op. cit., p. 10.

127. *Activities of Transnational Corporations in Southern Africa...,* op. cit., p. 45.

128. Rothmyer and Harrell, "South Africa Fact Sheet," op. cit., pp. 2-3.

129. *Activities of Transnational Corporations in Southern Africa...,* op. cit., p. 63.

130. Ibid.

131. Murphy, Caryle. "S. Africa Offers Lures to Its Blacks," *Washington Post,* March 13, 1980.

132. Ibid.

133. Office of the General Counsel, Equal Employment Opportunity Commission, January 10, 1980; *Pension Investments: A Social Audit.* New York, Corporate Data Exchange, Inc., 1979. (The CDE listing also includes enforcement actions by the Office of Federal Contract Compliance of the U.S. Department of Labor. The OFCC monitors the equal employment compliance of federal contractors and subcontractors.)

134. Excerpts from the testimony of Randall Robinson, Executive Director of TransAfrica, in: *United States Private Investment in South Africa,* op. cit., p. 427.

135. Murphy, Caryle. "S. Africa Offers Lures to Its Blacks," op. cit.

136. Ibid.

137. Wiehahn, Nicholas. Quoted in: "Comments on the Business Codes," *South African Outlook,* vo. 109, no. 1295, May 1979, p. 70.

138. "Apartheid for 'Industrial Peace'." The Washington Office on Africa, op. cit., pp. 2-3.

139. Ibid., p. 3.

140. Myers, op. cit., p. 31.

141. Thatcher, Gary. "Apartheid: Changing Form ... But Not Effect?" *Christian Science Monitor,* July 10, 1979.

142. Johannesburg Advice Office of the Black Sash, op. cit., p. 1.

143. Murphy, Caryle. "Pass System: Daily Affront to Black South Africans," *Washington Post,* August 23, 1979.

144. Zulu Chief, Gatsha Buthelezi, quoted in: "Apartheid for 'Industrial Peace'," op. cit., p. 4.

145. "South Africa Rules Out One Man, One Vote Forever," *New York Times,* November 11, 1979.

146. Black Sash Report: 1979. "Black Frustration in Face of Implementation of Plural Relations Amendment Act of 1979."

IPS PUBLICATIONS

South Africa:
Foreign Investment and Apartheid
By Lawrence Litvak, Robert DeGrasse, Kathleen McTigue

A critical examination of the argument that multinationals and foreign investment are a force for progressive change in South Africa. This study carefully documents the role that foreign investment has played in sustaining apartheid. $3.95.

Black South Africa Explodes
By Counter Information Services

The only detailed account available of events in South Africa in the first year since the uprising which began in June 1976 in Soweto. The report exposes the reality of life in the African townships, the impact of South Africa's economic crisis on blacks, and the white regime's dependence on European and American finance. $2.95.

Buying Time in South Africa
By Counter Information Services

An update of events in South Africa since 1976. Despite a severe recession, continuing struggle and external criticism, the South Africa state has reaffirmed and increased its control. Supported by world banks, multinationals and governments with an economic stake in South Africa, the racist regime is implementing the "grand apartheid" by eliminating all blacks through the creation of home states. $2.95.

The Politics of National Security
By Marcus G. Raskin

This historical analysis of the national security state traces its evolution from a planning instrument to ensure national stability, mute class conflicts and secure the domestic economy to the basis for covert and overt imperialism. The debacle in Indochina, the genocidal nature of the arms race, and growing economic instability, however, signal the decline of this structure. This incisive study impels renewed public debate of national policy and purpose. $5.95.

Peace In Search of Makers
Riverside Church Reverse
the Arms Race Convocation
Jane Rockman, Editor

A compilation of papers denouncing the proliferation of sophisticated weaponry, which threatens a nuclear cataclysm and destroys our society by diverting resources from social services and programs. This volume confronts the moral, economic, strategic and ethical aspects of the arms race and appeals for a citizen coalition to reverse the course of social decay and uncontrolled nuclear armament. Contributions by Richard Barnet, Michael Klare, Cynthia Arnson, Marcus Raskin and others. $5.95.

NEWLY REVISED! The Counterforce Syndrome:
A Guide to U.S. Nuclear Weapons
and Strategic Doctrine
By Robert C. Aldridge

An identification of how "counterforce" has replaced "deterrence" as the Pentagon's prevailing doctrine, contrary to what most Americans believe. This thorough summary and analysis of U.S. strategic nuclear weapons and military doctrine includes descriptions of MIRVs, MARVs, Trident systems, cruise missiles, and M-X missiles as they relate to the aims of a U.S. first strike. $4.95.

The Giants
Russia and America
By Richard Barnet

An authoritative, comprehensive account of the latest stage of the complex U.S.-Soviet relationship; how it came about, what has changed, and where it is headed.

"A thoughtful and balanced account of American-Soviet relations. Barnet goes beyond current controversies to discuss the underlying challenges of a relationship that is crucial to world order."—Cyril E. Black, Director, Center for International Studies, Princeton University

"An extraordinarily useful contribution to the enlightenment of the people of this country .... It is of fundamental importance that we understand the true state of our relations with Russia if we are to avoid a tragic mistake in our future."—Senator J.W. Fulbright. $4.95.

Dubious Specter: A Skeptical Look at the 'Soviet Threat'
By Fred Kaplan

A thorough exposition and analysis of the myths and realities surrounding the current U.S.-Soviet "military balance." Kaplan's comparisons of U.S. and Soviet nuclear arsenals and strategies provide the necessary background for understanding current debates on arms limitations and rising military costs. $4.95.

The Rise and Fall of the 'Soviet Threat': Domestic Sources of the Cold War Consensus
By Alan Wolfe

A timely essay which demonstrates that American fear of the Soviet Union tends to fluctuate due to domestic factors, not in relation to the military and foreign policies of the USSR. Wolfe contends that recurring features of American domestic politics periodically coalesce to spur anti-Soviet sentiment, contributing to increased tensions and dangerous confrontations. $4.95.

Resurgent Militarism
By Michael T. Klare and the Bay Area Chapter of the Inter-University Committee

An analysis of the origins and consequences of the growing militaristic fervor which is spreading from Washington across the nation. The study examines America's changing strategic position since Vietnam and the political and economic forces which underlie the new upsurge in militarism. $2.00.

Toward World Security: A Program for Disarmament
By Earl C. Ravenal

This proposal argues that in light of destabilizing new strategic weapons systems and increasing regional conflicts which could involve the superpowers, the U.S. should take independent steps toward disarmament by not deploying new "counterforce" weapons, pledging no first use of nuclear weapons, and by following a non-interventionist foreign policy. $2.00.

Conventional Arms Restraint:
An Unfulfilled Promise
By Michael T. Klare and Max Holland

A review of several aspects of current steps to reduce the amounts and sophistication of weapons sold, close loopholes in Carter administration policy on overall sales, especially to human rights violators, reduce secrecy, improve Congressional oversight, limit co-production arrangements and restrict sales of police and related equipment to authoritarian regimes abroad. $2.00.

Myths and Realities
of the 'Soviet Threat'
Proceedings of an IPS Conference
on U.S.-Soviet Relations

Distinguished experts explore the prospect for change in the USSR, define the role of the Soviet military in Eastern Europe and assess the U.S.-Soviet military balance. Based on reliable data and analytical rigor, these statements debunk the myth of a new Soviet threat. $2.00.

The New Generation
of Nuclear Weapons
By Stephen Daggett

An updated summary of strategic weapons, including American and Soviet nuclear hardware. These precarious new technologies may provoke startling shifts in strategic policy, leading planners to consider fighting "limited nuclear wars" or consider a preemptive first strike capability. $2.00.

Postage and Handling:
All orders must be prepaid. For delivery within the USA, please add 15% of order total. For delivery outside the USA, add 20%. Standard discounts available upon request.

Please write the Institute for Policy Studies, 1901 Que Street, N.W., Washington, D.C. 20009 for our complete catalog of publications and films.